THE BASEMENT BOOK

THE BASEMENT BOOK

UPSTAIRS DOWNSTAIRS:
RECLAIMING THE WASTED SPACE IN YOUR BASEMENT

■

Tom Carpenter
& Jeff Taylor

■

Technical illustrations by Roberta Cooke
Front cover and opening illustrations by Brad Sneed

Houghton Mifflin Company
Boston New York

For information about permission to reproduce selections from this book, write to
Permissions, Houghton Mifflin Company, 215 Park Avenue South,
New York, New York 10003.

Library of Congress Cataloging-in-Publication Data

Carpenter, Thomas.
    The basement book : upstairs downstairs: reclaiming the wasted space in
your basement / by Tom Carpenter and Jeff Taylor; illustrated by Brad
Sneed and Roberta Cooke.
         p.   cm.
    Includes index.
    ISBN 1-881527-99-9 (softcover)
    1. Dwellings—Remodeling—Amateurs' manuals. 2. Basements—Remodel-
ing—Amateurs' manuals.
I. Taylor, Jeff (Jeff Damon) II. Title.
TH4816.3.B35C37 1996
643'.5—dc20   95-48348

Designed by Pamela Fogg

DOC 10 9 8 7 6 5 4 3 2

ACKNOWLEDGMENTS

PEOPLE WHO WRITE SUCH BOOKS AS this one are usually passing on information they learn from others. We are no exceptions to the rule; we didn't make up any of what follows. Most everything we know we learned the hard way, by having someone wiser tell us what to do, then ignoring that good advice until some laughable screwup illustrated why we should have done it the way we were told.

Jeff would like to acknowledge his lifelong debt to Burdell Swanson and to all the others who once took the time to teach a Hippie (as they called them then) college kid about the Real World of carpentry. Tom would like to thank both Geoff McKay and John Boxtel, whose workshops and job sites he visited more than once during the writing of this book, looking for quick clarifications and detailed explanations.

Thank you, Sandy Taylor and Emily Stetson, who, respectively, edited and copyedited the manuscript, and who between them made what was rough, smooth; what was confusing, clearer; and in a couple of places, what was purely wrong, right.

Thank you, Robbie Cooke, for the illustrations. At a thousand words per picture the drawings in this book have more to say than the text.

And finally, thanks to Joy and Debi, Beth, Serenity and Telfer, the ones we love.

■

This book is dedicated to anyone who has ever stood
in the middle of his or her basement floor, hands on hips,
eyebrows rising slowly, and thought,
Hey, this would make a good room for the kids.

■

CONTENTS

INTRODUCTION

AVING AN UNFINISHED FULL basement is like having an extra bungalow hidden beneath your house. Whether the walls of your basement are stone, poured concrete or cement block—maybe even modern pressure-treated plywood and framing—makes no difference. Whatever the number of square feet you have on the first floor, that's how many more you have waiting at the bottom of the basement stairs. A family room, a study, another bathroom, perhaps a games room with a full-sized billiard table, more closet space, a pantry, additional bookshelves, a quiet enclosure for the washer, dryer and furnace, even another soundproof paddock in which children can vanish for a few blessed hours—all of these wonderful places await the homeowner willing to spend the money and time necessary for conversion. No need to build an expensive addition or to sacrifice precious yard space, no

variances to obtain, no carefully waterproofed roof or insulated walls to erect, and absolutely no reason to wait for good construction weather. Just make the decision, plan the schedule, allocate the money and do it in your spare time, from the convenience of your own home. How perfect, how simple in theory.

All that extra area, however, is merely potential space; turning an unfinished basement into living area is not something you'll do in a weekend or even in a week. In fact, the planning phase (the most crucial stage of any project) will take much longer than a week. Obtaining permits, lining up materials and contractors and attending to the myriad details that come before the first nail is driven will probably suck up about as much energy as you'd planned to spend on the whole endeavor, and perhaps as many hours. God, as they say, is in the details, and a construction project like this is *all* details, a process as delicate and dovetailed as building a ship in a bottle. Reading up on what you need to know now will save you sleepless nights later on.

■ C O N S I D E R I N G
T H E
P R O S   A N D   C O N S ■

THE SMARTEST THING YOU CAN DO first is to sit down with paper and pencil and a calculator, or a good architectural computer drafting/estimating program, and get your three-dimensional dream down in two dimensions, with lots of numbers and dollars spelled out to the last digit and penny. These estimates will all change, probably in the upward direction, but for now you must try to contain costs. Luxuries come later, when you've safely paid for everything that you didn't plan on paying for. In other words, don't run out and buy a new billiard table yet: You may need that money for a toilet in the bathroom. Set your priorities in stone and have them bronzed, or you'll wind up with an unfinished headache that no amount of aspirin can relieve. Remember that time only *seems* to be flexible (as when you're having fun or visiting the dentist). A job for which you have allowed a day will in all likelihood take two or three, and then only if everything goes perfectly—which it won't.

Note, at this point, how your house and life have attained an equilibrium based on long use and inertia. Examine the state of your home life and the condition of your own mental health. Now ask yourself if you are willing to gamble everything by introducing the chaos of construction into your orderly universe.

On the plus side of the ledger, you stand to improve your domicile considerably, increasing not only its dollar value but its utility and comfort. With a wave of your hand, you will be able to dismiss your thundering, shrieking children to the nether regions until you are strong enough to bask in their presence once more, or abandon the upstairs to them and retire with your spouse to the warm and quiet family room downstairs for a leisurely cup of coffee. The next time company drops in, you will have a well-stocked pantry, perhaps even a cool wine cellar, and your company will depart well-fed and glowing but muttering with admiration and ill-disguised envy all the way back to the cramped, wretched warren *they* call home.

Sounds lovely, doesn't it? But in the interest of a fair presentation, the authors will admit the following. We have done much construction in our respective lives, and our experience has been enlightening. We know firsthand what it feels like to embark on a large remodeling voyage into the unknown, and how quickly calm confidence can turn into stark terror. We know how a blueprint that is microscopically exact one day can become a mass of lies the next, useful only for swatting flies. We know what it feels like to arrive at the presumed end of a midnight project such as painting a new wall and to use up the last few seconds by hanging a picture, and how easily the nail can find an unprotected copper pipe containing oceans of water exploding forth in a torrent, and how the next day dawns on a sobbing wreck that used to be a sane human being. We have made these and other, even worse, mistakes in judgment. For that reason, we will not cruelly delude you with words like "easy" and "simple" without a disclaimer that you may take as a warning: Where such words appear in this book, substitute "potentially difficult" and "possibly disastrous." Furthermore, while religion is not in our purview, we counsel you that there may be times to pray for a miracle. If you make a mistake at a critical juncture and do not have the wisdom to recognize it, and if you blithely keep building in the hopes that everything will work itself out, God help you.

That said, remodeling a basement is easy and simple. Make a schedule of steps to be taken, budget your time and money wisely, spend many hours in your basement looking around and visualizing, write down the phone numbers of any contractors you wish to employ or may need in an emergency, shop around for the best prices on materials and begin the work. Eventually you will come to the end of it.

Many things will occur in the interim (not all of them welcome), but with perseverance and luck, your ugly unfinished basement will evolve into a thing of beauty. Put film in your camera and take pictures before, during and after, and someday you will show them to guests who will marvel at your unsuspected talents. Write down every detail of the work in a notebook; save all your receipts; learn to make lists. Do not continue working past the point of exhaustion, and get plenty of rest and good food during the actual construction phase. Above all, decide in advance not to despair or scream at your loved ones. Write down that resolution and post it on the wall. Speak softly and clearly to *everyone*—family, friends, suppliers, contractors and clerks—and proceed as if everything is under your control. Cultivate patience. Recite this mantra: *Rome was not built in a day, but it's still there.*

▪ D O I N G T H E R I G H T T H I N G ▪

INCLUDED IN THE GROUP OF PEOPLE TO whom you will be speaking softly and with great deference is the building inspector. This is the person within the local building department who can help you design and build your basement to code, approve your sketched plans and guide you through the morass of paperwork that lies between you and the permits you'll need in order to change your basement from unfinished to livable. This is also the person who can post a stop-work notice on your front door and withdraw your certificate of occupancy for noncompliance; the person who can force you to spend more money making your basement safe according to code; the person who can make you tear out weeks of work and do it over correctly. In short, the person who can make your life more difficult than you would *ever* have dreamed possible.

Understandably, many people are so uneager to make the acquaintance of this person that they fail to notify him or her that anything is going on in their lives, basement-wise. After all, the work is taking place inside—unless you are excavating for new drainpipe, setting new windows or installing rain gutters—and it is very tempting to do an end run, saving time, money and hassles by doing everything *sub rosa*.

But remember that insurance companies look askance at work that has not been inspected by building inspectors, perhaps sucking back their insurance coverage with a cancellation notice. It's wise to check with them beforehand, because your coverage may not be in force without a special construction rider. In other words, they can refuse to pay claims for damage and/or injury incurred while remodeling, especially if the work falls under the heading of "illegal" (that is, done without proper permits). And even though the electrical and plumbing inspectors may work in different buildings, these people have one another's telephone number. Most electricians will not work in the absence of permits, nor will most plumbers: If you hire them, they may obtain the permits themselves, and in fact may be required to do so on pain of losing their licenses. And there goes your secret project. A million bureaucrats will descend on you, imposing heavy fines, and any money or hassles you thought to save will be multiplied tenfold.

For these and other reasons, we strongly recommend that you bite the proverbial bullet and go down to your city, county or local building department with a sketch of your proposed remodeling project and a checkbook and do the right thing. In the long run, you will be happier. And so will your insurance agent.

▪ T O O L S . . . L I G H T S . . . A C T I O N ! ▪

IF YOUR GARAGE OR UNFINISHED BASE-ment already has a workshop, fine. You'll have a location in which to store all your tools, including rentals; a worktable and vise where you can cut pipe, wood members and molding; a place to clean drywall trowels and paintbrushes; and maybe an area where much of the mess—but not all of it, oh no!—can be segregated. The chaos will spread soon enough, but in the beginning you'll always be able to find a specific tool.

If you do not have such a workplace, set aside a well-lighted area with an old table or bench and establish a beachhead for your main assault. Inasmuch as it's possible, attempt to keep tools in the same place, and return them to that place after use, even when you're sure you'll be able to find them in the place you used them last. Take our word for it: You won't. A crowbar, for example, will quickly vanish in the midst of the same construction debris it has created. We know of one remodeler who discarded his favorite crow by accident. One night, he left it in a wheelbarrow full of ancient ceiling tiles, intending to retrieve it the next morning; instead, he emptied the wheelbarrow into the giant metal refuse bin he had rented, and the truck came early that morning to empty it. By the time our friend began his search, his favorite crowbar was on its way to the county landfill. And this is not an isolated case. We have lost tools in exactly the same way.

Having a workshop or work area also allows you to clean and oil tools or change blades as needed. A pipe wrench that is rusty and wet is no fun to use, and it doesn't work as well, either. A dull power saw not only does not cut well, it's also dangerous. A table or workbench provides a nice flat surface on which to store, repair and maintain all your tools. A light source, either overhead or clamped onto the table, makes them easy to see. Most basements are a little under-illuminated anyway, and in the course of moving pipes and wires around, you will probably disconnect much of your overhead lighting. Round up a couple of transportable trouble lights and place them strategically in your work area before you need them.

Now think in terms of overall lighting for the job at hand. We like to be able to see what we are working on, even if everything is fairly visible, so we both own portable halogen lights that virtually flood a given area with photons. For exacting work such as plumbing and wiring, the advantages of being able to see the work clearly, without straining or squinting, cannot be overstated (although we'll try). Jeff once sweated a copper pipe joint by flashlight, meaning without sufficient ambient light to ensure that the solder had made a good bond on the back side of the elbow, which it had not. As a result, he was forced to spend a full three hours driving to

town to get a new elbow and reinstalling the damn thing, this time in the bright glare of a halogen worklight. Thereafter, he has never plumbed anything without a good light nearby. And he never will again.

·TO CONTRACT, SUBCONTRACT OR DO·IT·YOURSELF·

IF YOU HAVE THE SKILLS AND TOOLS necessary to completely refinish your own basement (including wiring and plumbing and maybe a new heat pump), to finish drywall seamlessly, to paint or stain everything without spilling more than you apply and to lay flooring (carpet, tile, vinyl)—all to professional standards—you probably have done it many times before. You have decades of experience and thousands of dollars invested in tools. Stop here: You don't need to read this book.

The authors have worked in construction for so many years and in so many places that we aren't afraid to offer opinions about professional contractors as a breed. Ninety percent of all contractors are good at what they do, 4% are learning from their (basic) mistakes and will do better after they have more experience, another 3% will *almost* be experts after their next job (maybe working on your house), 2% are mildly dishonest with themselves and their customers and 1% are crooks who should be remodeling their own jail cell with a mop and a bucket of water.

Statistically, then, the odds are good that you can find a contractor or a number of contractors who will do the work competently and charge you a fair price. Why, then, do you hear and read so many horror stories about ripoff artists and traveling construction grifters? Because they get around, they have a good spiel and they offer prices too good to be true. The unwary homeowner tells everyone in earshot, and each of those people repeats the story to a handful of friends, and so it goes until it seems the entire world must be filled with unscrupulous builders. By contrast, the reliable, competent and reasonably priced contractor will get no more than a reference, and then only if someone asks. A job that is done correctly is so common as to be unremarkable. After paying a hefty bill for a lot of expert work, most homeowners don't give it another thought. A glowing reference may be deserved, but it's not always offered; if an appropriately businesslike contractor wants recognition, he or she usually prefers it in the form of prompt payment.

So when a neighbor or friend recommends a contractor, and when that contractor is licensed and bonded (be sure to check, including other references; no reputable contractor will be offended), you can be confident that this person will do a good job for a fair price.

By the same token, when you hire a door-to-door contractor who just happens to be passing through the area—someone who will work for cash if you don't need a written estimate, someone who will need to borrow or rent tools—rest assured you will pay too much. You would be unwise to pay them *any* amount in advance, and you will probably be unhappy with what you pay upon completion.

If you *do* hire a contractor, be sure to get written estimates of both time and money, and be prepared to pay some cash in advance and regular amounts as work proceeds. Tell the contractor how involved you do (or in some cases, don't) want to be in the planning and supervision of the unfolding events, and be sure to speak your mind clearly and politely and regularly so that there is no possibility of you suffering in frustrated silence and then blowing up at this person who holds the fate of your home in his or her hands.

If you decide to forego a contractor, keep in mind that contractors earn their money by knowing enough about the building industry to intelligently coordinate the efforts of all the so-called subtrades: plumbers, electricians and so on. If you want to be your own contractor, be prepared to spend time acquiring some of that same expertise yourself. Ask lots of questions, read and spend evenings digesting what you learn. If your plans for the next day or weeks make sense to you, you'll be better able to stay calm and navigate the sea of construction. *Bon voyage!*

GETTING IT STRAIGHT (IN YOUR HEAD)

■

*Planning, Preplanning
and More Planning
Are the First Half of the Job*

W E KNOW SOMEONE WHO DRYWALLED OVER his primary gate valve. That's the main valve, the one that shuts off all the water to the house. He planned to return later and put in a hatch, but in the meantime, he drove a nail through a copper pipe (something else that got hidden behind the drywall), and instead of cutting a dainty trap door, he found himself clawing down clumps of gypsum board with the wrong end of a hammer head, trying to remember exactly where the valve was before the room flooded. The whole thing was a failure of planning. He never should have covered the valve; he should have marked the location of those pipes on the floor before the drywall went on; he should have taken a few Polaroid snapshots. He did none of these things. He's like the rest of us.

Planning is the root of efficiency. Time spent preparing for a project as complicated as a basement renovation pays off in time and materials saved later. It also does away with the need for clever *ad hoc* solutions to all those problems that crop up because you did not...make plans.

There are many uses for refinished basement space, but first you must convert the underground crypt and junk catchall into a clean, well-lighted place. And that means that before you raise a finger, you need to picture how you want things to turn out and then imagine *exactly* how you are going to make that happen. You can drop thousands of dollars into a basement and have little to show for it if you don't make careful, detailed plans, right down to what kinds of nails and screws you will need to handle every task.

Ensuring that your basement is dry and will remain that way can be a major undertaking in itself. Chapter Two deals entirely with the ways of moisture; in some houses, the lion's share of the work of a basement renovation will be taken up with water control. Once that is done, you need to examine the mechanical systems: Count them and take notice of exactly where they are located. You can do this planning yourself—it is mostly a matter of common sense—but don't hesitate to call in a professional plumber or electrician if you have any doubts or questions. We say it now and will repeat it throughout this book: Even paying for a professional's advice alone is money well spent. In some cases, these people will be able to make sense of complicated codes and tell you where you can take perfectly legal shortcuts and under which circumstances you may want to exceed the minimums of the American *Uniform Building Code* or the Canadian *National Building Code.*

Remember, your basement has been used to segregate the mechanical components of your house (plumbing, heating and wiring) from the living area upstairs. These components are fully visible in the basement, which keeps things simple, but after you change this area to living space and hide all the machinery away, you will still need to have access to pipes and wires and furnace filters for repair or maintenance.

For this reason, we strongly recommend taking lots of photographs before you begin and making notations as you go. Keep a construction log and fill it with notes and reminders and plenty of sketches (see Fig. 1). This will serve as a memory jogger should you require one a few years down the road. (Was the hot water pipe on the left or on the right? Did the wiring for the clothes dryer pass between these two joists or those two? A photograph and/or a sketch will tell you.) Be sure to date everything and to record changes as they occur.

▪ MAPPING THE MECHANICALS ▪

BEGIN YOUR RENOVATION PLANNING BY mapping the mechanical systems as they exist before any changes. Include plenty of measurements. Then begin to consider how you are going to tuck all the machinery into the new walls and ceilings of your proposed living space. Some mechanical components (pipes running parallel to joists, for instance) will be easy to cover over; others, such as a heating system, may have to be isolated with partitions.

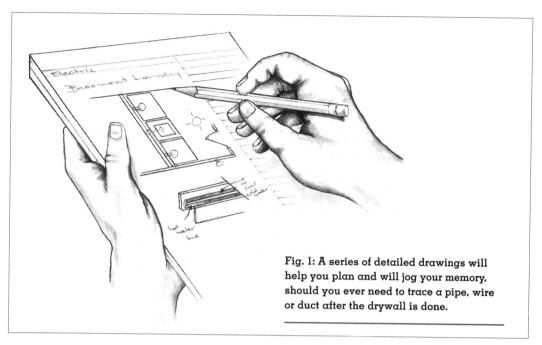

Fig. 1: A series of detailed drawings will help you plan and will jog your memory, should you ever need to trace a pipe, wire or duct after the drywall is done.

In case you have any doubts that, in planning, one thing leads to another equally important thing, consider the following: If you have a vertical 4-inch or 6-inch cast-iron pipe leading from the existing toilet to the septic tank or sewer system, and if your upstairs bathroom is located in the center of the house (as it often is), you should plan on building a wooden box or plumbing chase for this pipe (see Fig. 2) or incorporating it into a new basement wall. Unless you are prepared to move your entire bathroom, it is not always feasible to relocate this pipe, so it becomes an immutable constraint—just as much a condition of your planning as the foundation walls themselves (remember that the cleanout will have to be accessible, too).

If you construct a bathroom in the basement, it will probably be best to incorporate the existing soil pipe into a "wet wall" (a wall with 2x6 or 2x8 studs that can also accommodate your downstairs plumbing, the supply and waste pipes—all the "wet" stuff). The wet wall will then form one side of the new bathroom, and to minimize the amount of plumbing you have to do, you'll also want to locate the tub and sink against that wall, all of which means that that innocent-looking soil pipe in your empty basement ends up dictating both the location and floor plan of your new bathroom. On the other hand, it may be easier to simply frame a false pilaster around the pipe, with a hatch to provide access to the cleanout, and to locate a new bathroom elsewhere. This is the kind of decision that a licensed plumber can help you make.

Locate any secondary valves on the plumbing and consider whether you will ever need access to them. For example, will you ever want to stop the flow of water to just the upstairs bathroom so you can change faucet washers? Does a single pipe lead to an outside

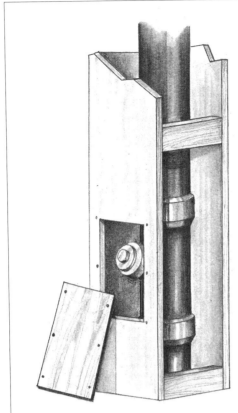

Fig. 2: When enclosing soil pipes, make sure you leave a hatch for the clean-out.

faucet that you'll want to shut off in the winter to prevent damage from freezing?

You also want to preserve your ability to switch power on and off, which means that the main electrical panel must remain accessible; certainly don't cover it with drywall, but don't plan to bury it in the darkest closet, either. It *can* be moved, but only at a significant cost of money and effort; you should probably plan around it.

The same goes for all the other machines now stashed in your cellar: the furnace, the heat recovery ventilator, the central vacuum, the water heater, water filters, the sump pump, burglar alarm panels, humidistats—anything. Locate these before you start, and make your plans with them in mind.

Like the plumbing stack, the furnace usually stays where it is and plans are made around it. You will need to build it a room of its own, allowing enough space to get at all sides for maintenance and to slide the filters in and out. Furnace ducts, on the other hand—although they may look pretty permanent hanging beneath the floor joists right at head level—can often be moved out of the way to the sides of the rooms you plan. A heating, ventilation, air conditioning (HVAC) contractor can quickly tell you how much the job will cost. Examine the ducts to see if there are shutoffs on any of them, then decide whether or not you will ever need to use those dampers to regulate the flow of warm air in your house.

Along with the main ductwork, the ceiling space of a basement almost always contains a host of wires and pipes and secondary ducts. Before you can frame the walls and interior partitions, before you can plan where to put the pool table or sofa, before you can really get into the fun part of converting your basement into a living space, you must attend to the ceiling.

If your basement has 9-foot ceilings, rejoice. The original builder was obviously thinking ahead, planning for the day when this (your) basement would become living space. This construction genius must have loved you like a son or daughter, because 9-

foot ceilings on basements cost quite a bit more than the typical 8-foot (or less) ceilings found in most basements. That extra foot means you can conceal all your ductwork, pipes, wires and drains below the joists but still above the finished ceiling. Flush-mounted light fixtures can be hidden in there, too. Happy day, you've got 9 feet to play with! If, on the other hand, you have the typical 8 feet or less of headroom (like 98% of home-owners), well, sorry. Don't take it personally: It doesn't mean your builder didn't care for you. Things could be much worse.

Now, take a long look at the ceiling of your basement. Walk around the perimeter a few times, and see how many protrusions (pipes, wires, ducts, soffits, etc.) stick down beyond the plane defined by the bottom of the joists. This is called "visualization." What you want to do is fully imagine how the finished ceiling will look. (**Hint:** You would like it to look like a flat, uninterrupted expanse of drywall hanging over your head, though you may not be so fortunate.) This step should precede even the drawings you will need to make for remodeling permits and mechanical mapping.

It will not hurt to lie on your back on the basement floor—no kidding!—and take another look at your ceiling. We know a man who did this with a garage creeper (a mechanic's dolly), rolling around on his own basement floor and staring upward, memorizing the wires he would have to reroute, the joists he would need to drill for pipes, the ductwork he would have to enclose by soffiting. He carried a yellow carpenter's crayon

and made notes on the concrete floor, such as, "Drane s. 4 j-spcsm thn e. (w. of) bthrm. suppy." This meant, to him, that the drainpipe directly above the scribbled note would go south four joist spaces, then east beginning at a point just to the west of the bathroom supply pipe. Afterward, he was able to draw a complete plan of what he intended to do, ceiling-wise, just by reading his marks on the floor, without eyestrain. There is no convenient place to write notes on the ceiling (besides, you'd get a pain looking up to read them), but reading notes written on a basement floor is as easy as looking at your feet. You can try this method to see how it works, perhaps adding modifications such as using a plumb bob—a string with a pointy weight centered on it (see Fig. 3)—to place X's on your floor. (You can also amaze your friends with the extent of your arcane knowledge by devising new codes that only you can read.)

As you examine the ceiling and map its present contents, also try to figure out ways you can rearrange wires and pipes. In some cases, you'll be able to relocate them against walls or partitions, where overhead plumbing and wiring can be hidden between furring strips or studs. While you are at it, decide whether your current plumbing and wiring are sufficient to handle the increased load of the added basement living space. Or is this a good time to replace old steel pipe and cast iron with new copper water supply lines and ABS or PVC plastic drainage pipe?

Planned wisely, the spaces between joists are very useful for hiding plumbing and wiring from sight (see Fig. 4), as long as they

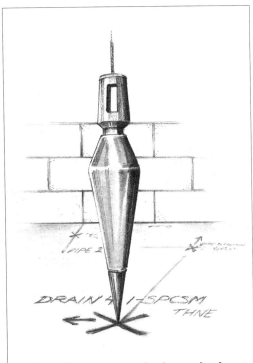

Fig.3: Gravity-operated, a brass plumb bob always points straight down, and is more reliable than a level.

run parallel to the joists. But when they run perpendicular, you have a problem that *cannot* be solved—and here is a stern word of warning—by simply cutting notches in your joists. (We'll discuss the "whys" in depth in Chapter Three.)

Even as you consider these complexities, broaden your investigation. A beam running the length of your basement might be high enough to allow the passage of a tall adult or so low that you will be forced to build a wall beneath with spaces cut out for doorways. Maybe wires and plumbing can be routed through that new wall. Will your staircase remain in its current location, or will it be

moved? The columns or posts that hold up the beam (or beams) may be movable, or they may not. And so it goes.

These and other issues must be addressed long before you drive a single nail or buy a single stud; before you even decide where the new rooms will go. Understand the parameters within which you will have to plan your renovation, then get out some graph paper and a pencil and start fitting together the pieces of what you want with the pieces that you've got. Once you've established what you're dealing with, the main thing is to get something down on paper to help you visualize the final result and to estimate costs. No one can scan an unfinished basement and rely on memory alone to solve all the problems that absolutely will come up once construction is underway.

▪ MAKING A LIST (AND CHECKING IT TWICE) ▪

NEXT, MAKE A LIST OF MATERIALS. Perhaps you intend to drywall your ceiling, for instance, after hiding all the mechanical things up between the joists and soffiting everything that won't fit without frustration. In that case, measure your basement ceiling and plan to order as many sheets of drywall as it would take to cover your ceiling if your ceiling had no protrusions such as soffits and beams, then add 20% to the order. (See Chapter Nine for complete details on how to estimate drywall.)

Perhaps you have decided to do the wiring yourself, or with the aid of an electrician who knows the things you do not (such as how to wire a three-way switch and divvy up the circuits for kitchen areas). Will you need to run more electrical wire? Then put a roll of wire on your list. Are you also going to do the plumbing yourself? Calculate how much copper pipe and ABS or PVC you'll need, including elbows, tees, reducers and unions. Plus solder. And flux. And propane cylinders. Not to mention bandages, burn ointment, safety glasses, rubbing liniment, aspirin and any tools we didn't mention (see Chapters Eight and Nine). And while you're at it, figure out how many shirts and pairs of pants you're likely to ruin. You can count on wrecking at least one of each while remodel-

ing. It sounds strange, but you might as well know the true cost of what you're up to. The addition Tom built last summer cost approximately $10,000 in materials and subtrades, plus one mangled fingernail, one trip to the hospital for a crushed thumb, half a dozen T-shirts rendered unfit for anything but more construction work and one totally blasted pair of shorts. He knows a man who used to do renovations for a living who included a pair of pants and a shirt on the itemized estimates he gave to customers.

Clairvoyance is not required (or, unfortunately, possible) during this phase of planning, but a little foresight will be almost as good: Many things can go wrong both during and after the renovation; assume that most of them will. *Plan* for them.

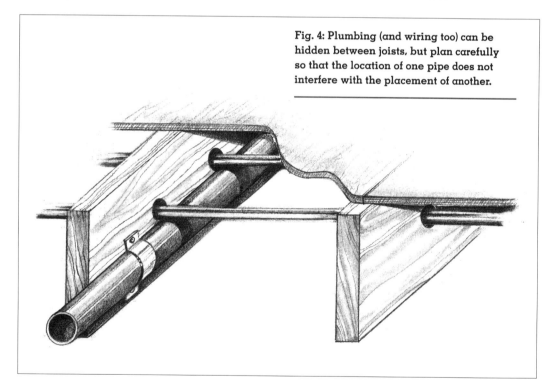

Fig. 4: Plumbing (and wiring too) can be hidden between joists, but plan carefully so that the location of one pipe does not interfere with the placement of another.

THE WATER CURE

■

*Long Before
You Can Install Drywall,
You Need Dry Floors*

BASEMENT RENOVATIONS SHOULD BEGIN ON THE roof, at the eaves. If you have moisture in your basement—and many people do, especially in older houses—then chances are good that rainwater collecting in the eaves is either overflowing because the downspout is plugged or falling through a leak in the gutter and then spilling next to your foundation. Contrary to popular assumptions, eaves troughs are not intended to keep water from falling on your head: They are installed to prevent water from soaking into the ground at your feet. If you have problems with your gutters, sort them out before you even take measurements for a basement project.

Wetness in basements causes several problems. Dampness can be uncomfortable: The cool moisture of a cellar in summer is just clamminess in other seasons. Moisture supports the growth of molds and fungi, whose spores can cause allergic reactions in some people and are suspected of being carcinogenic (they've been demonstrated to cause teratogenic mutations and birth defects in

mice, for example). The fungus that causes wood rot requires moisture to survive, and almost every building component from paint to drywall suffers in damp conditions. So before you invest labor and money in the downstairs of your house, dry it out and take steps to ensure that it will stay that way.

▪ D R A I N A G E
W O E S ▪

INSPECT YOUR BASEMENT CAREFULLY for signs of water stains, continuing seepage or damp spots, crumbling mortar and efflorescence (powdery or foamy white deposits on the concrete). If the evidence of moisture occurs well above the basement floor, the problem is likely caused by poor drainage of surface water or by window wells with insufficient drainage. Water lower down on the wall usually indicates other kinds of trouble.

Outside the house, the eaves troughs are definitely the most obvious problem, but they are not all that you need to investigate. Water collected from the roof funnels into the downspouts and is directed to the ground. From there, it must be moved away from the building (see Fig. 5). In many houses, the rainwater system empties into a storm sewer hookup, which is the ideal solution because the water then leaves the property entirely. In other situations, the gutter water may drain into a flexible plastic pipe that emerges from the ground beside the wall of the house. These pipes flow into the system that drains the footing (the long concrete pad that sup-

ports the basement walls). In the absence of either of these arrangements, any downspout should be connected to a horizontal length of pipe that carries the water several feet away from the foundation. These can be solid pipes or pipes with holes that distribute the water, or even collapsible plastic tubes that serve the same function. On older houses—although everything else may be working—that horizontal drainage may have been damaged by the lawn mower or flattened by the car or simply detached from the downspout. The link must be reestablished.

If your gutter and downspout system are in working order and you still have dampness soaking through the basement walls, it may have to do with unseen factors. The layers of pervious and impervious soils in your region, for example, may drain underground water toward your foundation. While building codes usually require proper underground drainage systems to handle all such problems, older houses may not be protected, and newer houses with poorly installed systems may be vulnerable, too.

A proper drainage arrangement allows any water near the foundation to percolate down to the level of the footing, where a clay or plastic or concrete drainage tile or pipe collects the water (see Fig. 6) and conducts it into a sewer or to an open drainage ditch or to a "dry well" (a gravel-filled hole located away from the house). If you have moisture seeping into your basement, you may need to have the foundation dug up and the drainage properly established.

The backfill material located right

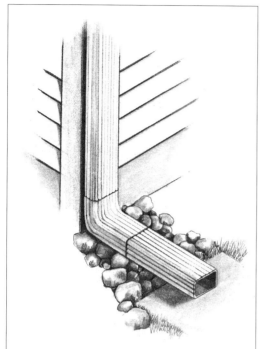

Fig. 5: The key to a dry basement begins on your roof. Downspouts can guide the water away from your foundation. Splash blocks work, as do perforated drainpipes.

way around the house. The panels are placed against the foundation, with their narrow channels facing out to provide a route for water. By using this system, you avoid the hassle of hauling away the soil you dig out and the cost of buying clean aggregate backfill. The panels, of course, also insulate the foundation, which is a big advantage, especially if you want to create living space in the basement. There are other systems you can use as well; a local building inspector can tell you which are approved for use in your area.

If you dig out your foundation, go all the way down to the footing. You should find perforated pipe, clay tiles or perforated flexible hose laid next to the building. If such drainage essentials are missing or are poorly installed, then that's likely your problem. Fix or replace them.

If you do end up digging out your foundation, check that the original builder covered the exterior with parging masonry (a thin coat of cement) and sealed it below grade with a waterproof bituminous coating (some form of smelly black tar). If either of those steps was neglected, do it now.

Trees growing against the house present another drainage problem. They look nice, but they're not a great idea. Fast-growing species are particularly bad because their roots can quickly make their way down to the footing—where water is supposed to collect—and disrupt pipe or tiles. Trees can also damage a foundation by becoming so large that they actually begin to push against the wall, especially if the soil is an unyielding clay. In the case of old stone foundations, roots can

against the foundation must be porous, and there cannot be any construction debris used as fill. Unfortunately, as tipping fees have risen at landfill sites, contractors have been known to bury construction waste right on the building site. Such materials tossed in next to the foundation can interfere with the movement of water down to the drains in the footing.

In some areas, building codes permit the use of grooved rigid blue polystyrene insulation for drainage purposes. These panels provide a solution to drainage woes that doesn't require you to dig out so wide a trench all the

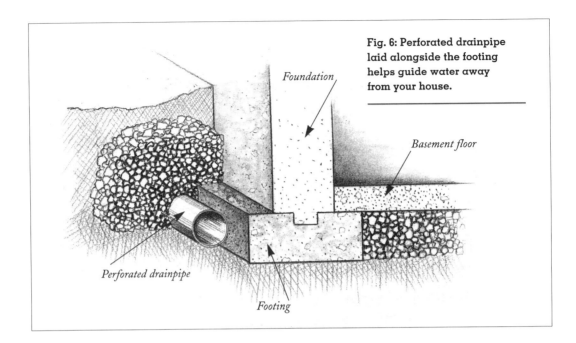

Fig. 6: Perforated drainpipe laid alongside the footing helps guide water away from your house.

Foundation

Basement floor

Perforated drainpipe

Footing

insinuate themselves into the wall itself.

If you are not the first owner of your house, you should take the presence of a sump (a large hole) and a sump pump in the basement as an indication that there may be flooding problems. Although a properly constructed sump is a perfectly acceptable way to drain the pipe or tiles laid along your footing, that is not the only reason a sump is built. It could also be there for unfortunate emergencies. If you have a sump in your basement, determine exactly what is draining into that hole before beginning any renovations.

The sump is usually located next to a perimeter wall. If there is drainage from the footing, there should be a pipe running into the sump from the direction of the foundation (see Fig. 7). Any other pipes leading to the sump will be connected to floor drains; you can sort out which is which by pouring water into the floor drains and seeing if it reaches the sump. If you find no line that runs in from the footing, consider carefully why your basement has been provided with a system designed entirely to drain water from the *floor*. If the drains that have been provided and the sump look as if they were built after the floor was poured, then you have clear evidence that your basement has flooded sometime in the past. You don't want to invest a lot of money in renovations until you've taken steps to ensure that your basement will never flood again.

It is possible in some regions for there to be water directly beneath your house. Under a certain amount of pressure, that water will be pushed slowly up through the concrete floor and into your basement. If the walls of your basement are dry, yet you have damp floors and have discovered (using the "aluminum foil test" [described on page 28; see also page 30, Fig. 9]) that the water is not condensation but is insidiously wicking up from below, you'll need to seal the concrete.

The problem with sealing a foundation from the inside can be illustrated with a sieve and a piece of plastic wrap. Imagine placing the plastic inside the sieve and then filling the sieve with water: Everything holds. Now imagine wrapping the plastic around the outside of the sieve and running water in: The water immediately pushes the plastic off the back of the mesh. A sealant on the inside of your basement is at a similar disadvantage.

Despite the difficulties of sealing from the inside, it is possible to stop water wicking up through concrete. The stickiest technique—and stickiness has a lot to be said for it in this context—is to slather on at least two coats of a bitumen (tar) product and then to put down a layer of polyethylene that is at least 6 mils thick. The concrete should be as dry as possible before doing this; judicious placement of a couple of large fans and even a dehumidifier will do a lot to prepare the surface. Sweep and vacuum like a maniac be-

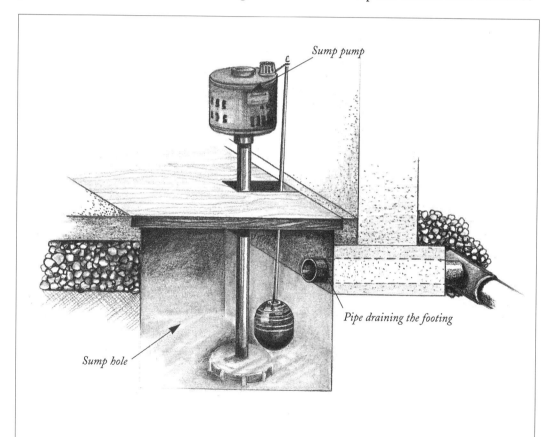

Sump pump

Pipe draining the footing

Sump hole

Fig. 7: Unless a sump and sump pump were installed to deal with flood waters *inside* the basement, there will be a pipe draining the footing into the sump itself.

fore you apply the coating.

Build a finished floor over the polyethylene, using wooden sleepers—a framework of 2x4s—and plywood (see Fig. 8). You cannot lay tile directly over poly, because the mastic or thinset cement won't adhere properly. (For specifics on laying sleepers, see pages 32-33 and 58-59.)

If you suspect you have such problems and are not happy with attempting to seal the concrete from inside, then it's probably time to call a contractor, because the only other solution is some fairly extensive and possibly very convoluted landscaping.

▪ C O N D E N S A T I O N   C O N C E R N S ▪

THE OTHER KIND OF MOISTURE PROBlem in basements has nothing to do with drainage. In the summertime, basements are cooler than the rest of the house and a good place to escape a heat wave. The underground space remains cooler because the temperature of the soil surrounding the basement walls rises only slowly through the summer months. The obvious difference in temperature, unfortunately, means that your cellar operates like a giant condensing coil during several months of the year.

Warm, moist summer air that makes its way to the basement strikes the cool walls and floor and leaves behind water in exactly the same way that droplets form on a cold drinking glass. Even if water isn't streaming down the walls, the air in the basement will have a higher relative humidity (RH) than upstairs. (Relative humidity is the term for the moisture present in the air, given as a percentage of the maximum amount of moisture the air can hold at that particular temperature.) The higher the RH, the damper the air in your basement will feel.

Unfortunately, the best solution to condensation problems involves the same mess of digging required to stop leaking. Insulating the *outside* of the basement walls makes the walls themselves part of the heated interior space of the house. The walls warm up in the winter, and in the spring the insulation prevents the cold soil from cooling the walls back down. Insulated walls tend to stay closer to the temperature of the interior of the basement, and that means much less condensation.

If you're not sure whether the moisture on your basement walls or floor is a result of seepage from the outside or condensation inside, do the following test. Tape squares of aluminum foil to damp spots on the floor and walls, and leave them there for a day or more. If there is moisture on the surface of the foil, your problem is condensation (see Fig. 9). If there is moisture on the floor or wall *beneath* the foil, it's seepage.

Other solutions to the problem of condensation dampness in your basement include simply installing a dehumidifier and/or shutting off the heating ducts to the rest of the house and using the furnace to provide a little bit of heat to the downstairs during the summer months. (The latter is a drastic measure, to be sure, if you've ever taken sanctuary in the cool cellar during a heat wave.) If

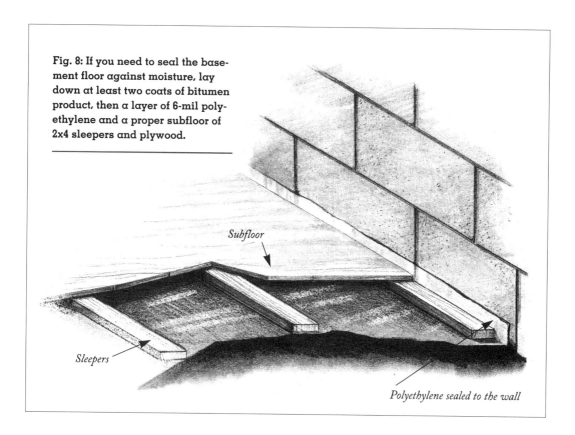

Fig. 8: If you need to seal the basement floor against moisture, lay down at least two coats of bitumen product, then a layer of 6-mil polyethylene and a proper subfloor of 2x4 sleepers and plywood.

Subfloor

Sleepers

Polyethylene sealed to the wall

possible, a dehumidifier should be set up on a little shelf near the laundry sink so that it can be left to drain continuously instead of having to be emptied every day. Or you can set up the dehumidifier over a floor drain, if you have one.

If your basement has had moisture problems of any sort—leakage or condensation—one of the first things you'll have to do is get rid of any mildew that has grown. Mildew thrives in moist conditions (the other place you find mildew in your house is the bathroom), and people tend to let it accumulate in seldom-used basement space. Because mildew reproduces itself, you want to eradicate it as completely as you can or it will soon be back.

The best way to be rid of mildew is sandblasting—no kidding. When Tom moved into his present house, there was a persistent mustiness in the downstairs; the space was damp and had been for decades. Because the foundation is stone and therefore awkward to wash, and because other renovations were taking place elsewhere in the house and already creating a desert storm of dust, he had the basement walls sandblasted. It took an hour. It cost about $150, and when he returned after it was done, he thought he'd made a dreadful mistake. The whole house stank of mildew. For several hours afterward he was convinced he'd unleashed a demon mold that was going to take over. When the air cleared, however, the basement walls were

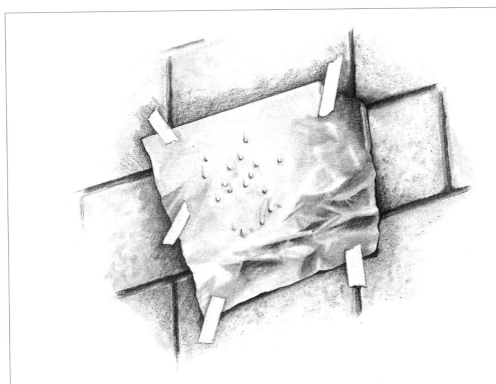

Fig. 9: To determine whether your moisture problems are due to condensation or seepage, tape a square of aluminum foil to the damp wall or floor for a day or so. Moisture on the surface means the problem is condensation.

as clean as new and the smell swept up with the sand and muck left behind by the blasting. If sandblasting seems like overkill, wash everything with a gentle solution of chlorine bleach and water.

There are architects who will insist that the idea of finishing a basement—a hole in the dirt beneath your house—is foolish. Usually their reasons have to do with wetness in that hole. They have a point. Stop everything and take care of any moisture problems before you proceed with costly changes to your basement space. The ongoing presence of moisture will degrade everything that you put in the basement, be it wooden studs, drywall, carpet or furniture. Dry everything out. Ensure that it will *stay* dry. Only then are you almost ready to start dreaming about what goes downstairs.

· RADON ·

FORTUNATELY, NEITHER OF US HAS A personal anecdote to tell about radon. We do not live in areas where radon poses significant problems. Even if we did, neither of us owns a house built to rigid contemporary standards of air-tightness. That same wind that blows right through and sucks up our costly heat also provides unintended anti-radon ventilation.

For many people, however, radon is a real problem. You can't smell it, you can't see it, yet there is a growing consensus among experts that the presence of this naturally occurring radioactive soil gas, even in moderate amounts, can significantly increase the likelihood of lung cancer. Having *any* radon in your house where it can be distributed by, for example, your heating system, is a problem that you should solve, but if you plan to convert the basement—where concentrations are potentially highest—into living space, you really must determine the levels of gas present and take appropriate steps.

To determine whether or not you have a radon problem, purchase a testing kit and follow the instructions. There are different types of tests, but each requires you to place the kit in the basement for a period of time and to then send it away for processing and interpretation. In some areas, building supply centers carry these kits; in others, you will need to contact a local health department (in Canada, a provincial Ministry of the Environment). The Canada Mortgage and Housing Corporation publishes material on radon and radon control; in the U.S., check with municipal inspectors and if necessary with a regional office of the Environmental Protection Agency.

Whether your basement has walls of poured concrete, cement block or stone, radon enters the basement through openings in the walls and floor, through cracks and deliberate holes alike. Plugging these holes or cracks can be done with cement and caulking and waterproof coatings or paints. In fact, imagine it is water you are trying to plug up, with the only difference being that radon will not force its way past patches the way water so often will. Use a hammer and a cold chisel (a steel chisel with a tempered edge) or even a grinder to widen narrow cracks so that whatever you use will "key" to the concrete. Polyurethane caulking is better than silicone for adhesion to concrete; use any of the spray foams to fill larger gaps. Clean all surfaces carefully before applying the caulking, even going so far as washing the area with a dilute muriatic acid solution or other etching products (available at hardware stores).

If you have a sump pump that receives runoff from the perimeter of the foundation (from outside the walls), you need to fit the sump hole with a sealing top and then check that any floor drains in your basement connected to that sump are fitted with proper traps to prevent the passage of gas. Because basement floor drains sit unused—with luck, for long periods of time—the water in a regular P-trap will often evaporate and gases will be free to pass. There are special self-sealing gas traps for such situations, available from plumbing supply houses.

In addition to cracks and the junction of walls and floor, look for all the deliberate holes in your basement walls—passages for buried power lines, dryer vents that go out below grade, plumbing lines, ground-source heating systems—anything that connects through the walls and may have a gap associated with it.

There are radon contractors in many areas where problems exist, but don't be intimidated and don't expect these people to possess arcane professional knowledge about radioactive gases. Radon is nothing more than a soil gas (one of many), and is caused by the breakdown of particles of uranium present in the dirt around your house. Since it seeps in through cracks and gaps in the floor and the foundation, radon control is a straightforward matter of minimizing the leakage—plugging the holes—and providing ventilation. A good contractor will be able to do these things with relatively little fuss and will also be able to tell you if any of the mechanical systems in your house is pulling air from inside the house and creating negative pressure that actually draws radon through the foundation and floor. A furnace that gets its combustion air from inside the house can do this, for example; so can a poorly balanced ventilation system or an oversized exhaust fan, such as the ones that suck down through a grill at the side of the stove.

In areas where there are serious levels of radon and first efforts to prevent its entrance to the house fail, the gas problem can also be dealt with by cutting through the basement floor and installing a pipe that extends from the gravel below the slab to an exterior wall or to the attic, along with a small fan that continually draws soil gases and exhausts them to the outdoors. In order for this technique to work, however, there must be an unbroken bed of gravel stretching under the entire base-

ment, which is something only the original contractor will know with certainty.

For the floor, you can also put down a layer of 6-mil plastic and either stick it directly to the floor, or at least seal the edges to the concrete walls or to an air-vapor barrier that you install behind any finish wall. Treat the matter as carefully as you would the installation of the air-vapor barrier itself and you should do fine. And, of course, ensure that the air-vapor barrier is also sealed somewhere up above so that there is no passage from behind the plastic back into the house.

Radon is important in its own right, but you also want to deal with it right away so you can make important decisions about floor coverings. Solutions to radon infiltration can limit your choices somewhat—you can't paint the concrete once you've covered it with plastic, for example—but lots of alternatives remain.

One is to set out a framework of 2x4s laid flat over plastic. These sleepers are there to provide nailers for a plywood subfloor. You set them down on their sides in order to preserve as much floor-to-ceiling headroom as possible and because with the plywood resting on the wider (4-inch) sides, you get that much more support. Treat the sleepers as you would a section of wall framing, laying them out on 16-inch centers and tying them together with the equivalent of a top and bottom plate. The sleepers should extend right to the floor's perimeter to support any new wall sections that you frame in and to give a nailing base at every edge. You can also place shorter pieces beneath the joints of the 4x8 plywood sheets you'll be laying (see page 59, Fig. 29).

Use shims to correct unevenness in the floor and to level the top surface of the sleepers. If the process of leveling raises the end of a sleeper, install more shims along its length every 12 inches or less: You want to be able to walk along the 2x4 without it bending under your weight. If there is play in the sleepers, there will be bounce in your floor, which can create noises, can wear on the plastic beneath and can disturb floor coverings such as tile or even seamless flooring. The top surface of the sleepers should meet the bottom surface of the subfloor perfectly.

When everything is arranged, fasten the sleepers in place with concrete nails, lead anchors or a proprietary system such as Tapcon screws or Hilti guns, which fire a fastener into the concrete with a charge the size of a .22. That oughta hold them.

THE MOVING PARTS

·

Deciding Where (or If)
You Should Relocate
the Machinery
in Your Basement

I N THE BASEMENTS OF RARE AND FORTUNATE PEOPLE, THE original builder, and everyone who came along after, installed each mechanical device in one corner of the building. The furnace is adjacent to the main electrical panel; the air conditioner is part of the heat distribution system; the air conditioner is part of the heat distribution system; and the heat recovery ventilator (HRV) is built right in. The hot water tank is there, too, and even the central vacuum has been tucked into the same strategic spot. In order to hide all these systems, you need only a soundproof door and a couple of walls to enclose the corner.

For the rest of us, however, the mechanicals in our basements are scattered all over the place. Concealing them means building half a dozen separate closets, each of which interferes with some better use of the space and introduces an element that must be accommodated by any new floor plan. Usually, the older the house, the worse the confusion. In Tom's house, for instance, the electric hot water heater and the electrical panel that supplies it occupy diago-

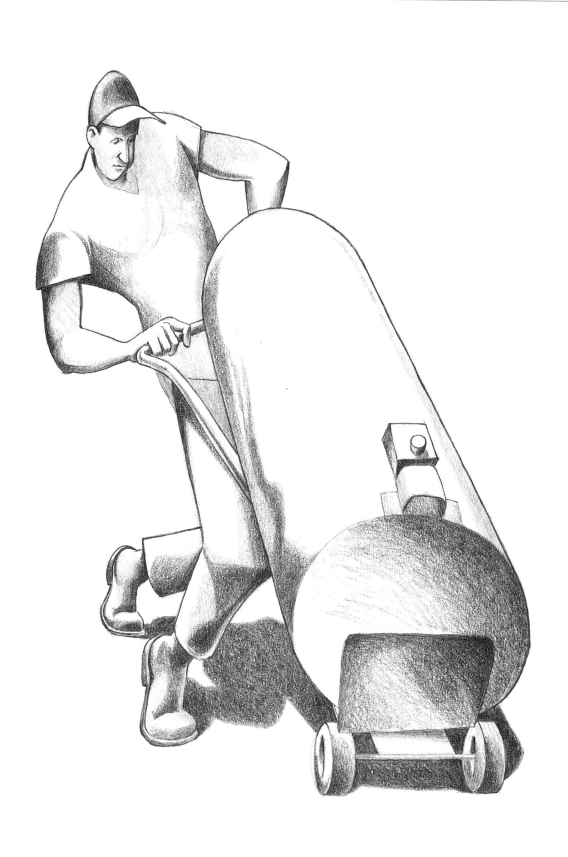

nally opposite corners of the basement. The furnace sits halfway down one side, the washer and dryer take up half of another side, and the main shutoff valve for water sits right down at floor level in a third corner.

Such cases leave you with some choices: You can build individual enclosures for each of these, or you can just live with things as they are and work around each machine in its turn. As another option, you can calculate just how much space you need and finish only half your basement, leaving all the obstacles in the unfinished half. Or you can work with some combination of these approaches. If none of these options suits your plans, you can gird yourself for extensive preparation work and join the rare and fortunate mechanically organized few by simply moving all the mechanicals into one area that can be easily enclosed.

But first, a warning: Old mechanical systems—furnaces, water heaters, old electrical panels (or small subsidiary panels sometimes called "pony boxes")—may be lined or insulated with asbestos. If such is the case in your basement, call a trained asbestos contractor to do the removal. These professionals employ a whole truckload of safety equipment, including special masks and vacuums and air-cleaning units. The certification required to work with asbestos varies from state to state and province to province, but if you have questions, call a local building inspector or health department or the nearest Environmental Protection Agency office.

Whether you move the mechanical systems or not, there are some basic operating

requirements to keep in mind when you plan to enclose the machinery. Almost all forced-air furnaces have some sort of filter between the cold air return and the furnace. The filters usually slide out the side of the cold air return, right where it connects to the furnace. You cannot locate a wall any closer to the furnace on that side than the full width of the filter or you won't be able to get the filter out. (Don't trust a measuring tape and your mental arithmetic for this kind of situation: Before you nail a wall in place next to the furnace, slide your filter all the way out, and make sure that you can then slide it back in again.) And no matter what kind of furnace you have, make sure there is room for a repairperson to get at the moving parts. Wherever there is a removable panel on the side of the furnace, leave enough space for a full-sized adult wearing a toolbelt to squat down comfortably.

The same applies to heat recovery ventilators (HRVs), which are a relatively new technology. These machines pump stale air out of the house through a series of corrugated panels that transfer warmth to the colder fresh air being brought in to replace it (see Fig. 10). The panels need to be cleaned periodically, and because they can freeze, they may need to be removed for thawing. So, like the furnace, the working side of the HRV must remain accessible with enough room to allow you to stand next to it while you do maintenance.

Hot water tanks also need attention occasionally. They, too, have small openings so that the heating elements can be changed and

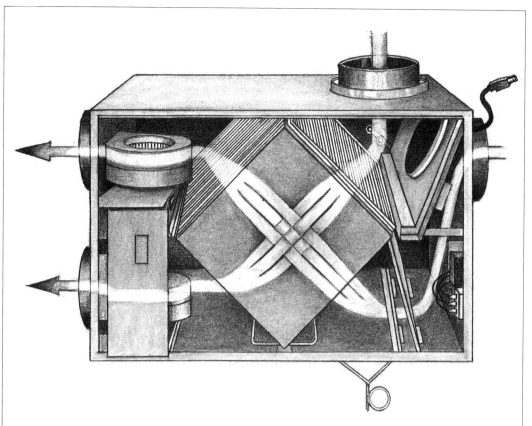

Fig. 10: Heat recovery ventilators (HRVs) save energy and money by extracting heat from stale air as it is being exhausted to the outdoors and transferring it to colder fresh air being brought in from outdoors. If an HRV is relocated, the side of the unit must remain accessible for cleaning and for those rare occasions when the panels freeze and must be thawed out.

the water temperature can be adjusted if necessary (see Fig. 11). You want to make sure that both openings, top and bottom, remain accessible. And because hot water tanks wear out every 10 years or so, you'll have to be able to remove the whole thing at some point. Don't block them into a corner from which they can't be extricated. A typical tank is under 2 feet in diameter, so you don't have to worry about getting it through the door of a new utility room, but you also don't want to

wedge it behind something like the central vacuum canister or the plumbing for the washing machine.

The electrical panel needs to be reachable as well, and since you may be looking for it in the dark (after, say, the circuit breaker for the basement has blown), you don't want to hide it away. **Note:** It is illegal in most places to enclose the main panel in a closet. When the firefighters come rushing in, they don't want to have to move aside clothes and your old yearbooks in order to extinguish the fire that is threatening to raze your hearth, home and chattel, too.

· M O V I N G
T H E
M E C H A N I C A L S ·

IF, FOR THE SAKE OF TIDINESS AND efficiency, you want to move some or all of the mechanicals into one corner of your basement, you need to plan carefully. Know what you are letting yourself in for. Each piece of machinery in your house is connected to something else, either by wires or water pipes or ductwork. Even the dryer has a flexible hose to exhaust damp air and its own special electrical outlet. Whatever you move will also have to take along all its attendant paraphernalia. In a couple of cases, it's just not worth the effort of moving all that stuff.

The electrical panel is probably the most immovable of all. It serves as the hub for wires in your house, and all roads lead to the one place where power enters from the utility pole or the buried cable outside. To move the main panel means not only rerouting dozens of wires, it also means having the utility company turn off the power to your house while you move the panel itself. This isn't work you can do yourself, and it costs a fortune to have it done. So forget it.

The furnace is just about as bad. Two sets of ducts converge on that one point: those that carry warm air away and those that return cold air. While ducts can be moved

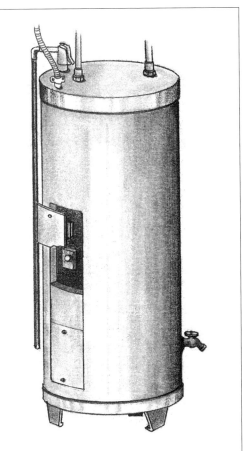

Fig. 11: A hot water heater is easily moved from one location to another, but the panels must remain accessible for servicing, and every 10 years or so the whole thing must be replaced.

somewhat, if you make drastic alterations, you risk changing the careful balance of the system, which means you may need an expert to reestablish equal flow to all areas of the house. Hot water furnaces are tricky, too. If your furnace is gas, you'll have to hire a licensed gas-fitter to reconfigure the supply pipes for you and you'll have to relocate the exhaust pipe—assuming you have a recent-model high-efficiency furnace and can reroute waste gases out through an adjacent wall. In older models, you may be prevented from moving the furnace because it requires a proper chimney and flue. Even if your furnace is a newer model, there are usually local regulations about the position of the exhaust pipe, which will limit your options. Tom can't have a gas water heater in his house, for instance, because there is nowhere to locate a vent that isn't too close to a window or door or existing air intake. When all is said and done, you probably don't want to move your furnace.

The remaining mechanical systems are more flexible, however. If you want to bring systems together, move these others to the same area as the furnace or the panel box. Although gas hot water heaters are usually as permanent as furnaces, an *electrical* hot water tank, for example, is quite straightforward. You turn off the electricity at the panel, disconnect the wiring from the tank, disconnect the water supply and outflow pipes, drain the tank so that it doesn't weigh a ton and then put it wherever you want it. Once you've relocated the tank and made sure it is level and stable, you simply hook up the cold water supply and the hot water outlet and reroute the wiring. If you live in the country and have a pump for the well and maybe a cold water tank, too, these can often be relocated with only a little rewiring and a bit of plumbing work. Similarly, washers and dryers can be shifted: You may need to reroute water supply lines and drains and wires, but the move can certainly be done with a little patience. Cen-

tral vacuum systems are even easier. The additional lengths of pipe you'll need are available in many plumbing supply houses and from retailers of the vacuum units. Then all you'll need is another source of power—a simple matter if you are moving all these appliances next to the main electrical panel.

Whatever you decide to move, keep it convenient. Don't opt for the false economy of fitting everything into the utility room like a Chinese puzzle. Take the space you need so that all this machinery can still be operated and serviced without extraordinary effort. Then soundproof the walls of the enclosed space so you won't have to hear or think about the "workings" of your basement. Best of all, you'll end up with a wide open space in the remainder of the basement that can be divided up into the living areas you want.

▪ HIDING THE TENTACLES (WIRES, PIPES AND DUCTWORK) ▪

AS YOU MAKE DECISIONS ABOUT where all the machinery is going to end up, keep in mind that you will have to hide away any pipes and wires that you reroute. While you are doing that, also plan to relocate any existing wires and pipes that stick down from the ceiling or that travel through a wall you have decided to remove or that currently snake their way across an exposed foundation wall that you plan to cover.

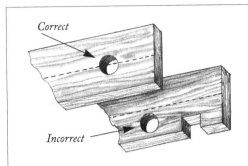

Fig. 12: Avoid notching your joists or putting a hole near the top or bottom; if you must make a hole, a circular opening through the center—the neutral axis—is best.

Start with the plumbing, as it's easier to run a wire around a pipe than vice versa. Now here's one of those stern warnings: When you make your preliminary examination of the pipes that you might want to move, *crush* your first impulse. *Do not notch the bottoms of your joists. Do not notch the bottoms of your joists. Do not notch the bottoms of your joists.* These joists are holding up your house, and it weakens them at the most critical point to notch the bottoms. Instead, drill holes through the center of the joists—the neutral axis—where the forces of tension and compression are balanced (see Fig. 12). Also make your holes just large enough to accommodate a pipe or wire.

Give some thought to the proposed bearing walls and wet walls (interior walls containing water pipes, both pressure lines and drains) and to the partitions. All make excellent hidey-holes for wiring and plumbing. If you have to run a wire in one direction, for example, it's easier to thread it through holes in the studs of an unfinished wall going in that same direction than it is to drill overhead through joists that are running perpendicular. Each basement is different; only you can figure out what will meet your needs. But be sure to ask the patient building inspectors, store clerks, consulting plumbers, electricians

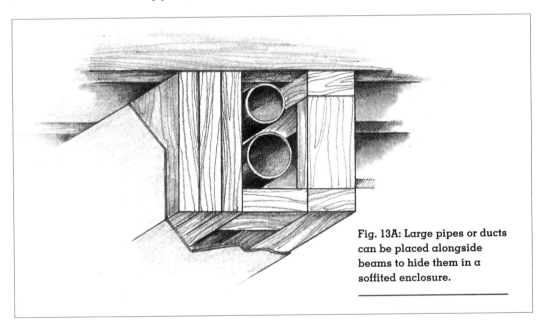

Fig. 13A: Large pipes or ducts can be placed alongside beams to hide them in a soffited enclosure.

and heating personnel about applicable building codes. The cleverest solution in the world is only a make-work project if it violates code, because you'll have to tear it out and do it over correctly.

Anything that can't be hidden away inside joists or walls will require you to build soffits. Basically, a soffit is a framed enclosure projecting down from the ceiling and surrounding anything from wiring and plumbing to heating ducts. (Let us pause here to warn you for the first time about enclosing heating ducts: If you have forced-air heating, then chances are that at least some of the warm air for your basement is simply blowing out of a louvered opening in the side of one of those large square heating ducts overhead. Do not cover up that opening.) If you have a bearing beam and an adjacent drainpipe running parallel, you may want to build a soffit big enough to enclose them both, provided, of course, that this leaves headroom to walk under it. Most often a soffit consists of a wood frame hanging from the joists on 2x4s (see Figs. 13 A and B for details of soffit construction). As you plan your soffits, keep in mind that once the 2x4s are fastened in place, you won't be able to hammer other members to those vertical ones. You will have to construct the entire soffit assembly on the floor, then raise it into place and spike it, or you will need a screw gun or a drill with a driver bit so you can screw the pieces together in place.

But now we're getting ahead of ourselves, because once you're ready to be installing soffits, you should also be planning the walls of your new basement layout and preparing to do the framing.

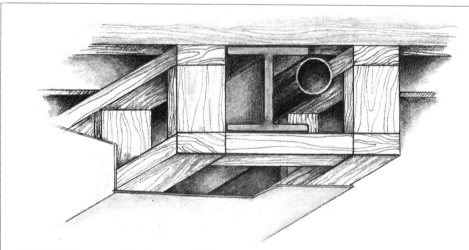

Fig. 13B: If support is being provided by a steel member, the entire I-beam will have to be enclosed. Large pipes can be placed inside the legs of an I-beam prior to soffiting, but be sure they do not touch the I-beam, to avoid conducting sound.

KINGS, STUDS AND JACKS

·

Meeting the Members of Your Framing Crew

MOST BASEMENTS HAVE FOUR OUTSIDE WALLS made of concrete block or poured concrete, and a reinforced concrete slab floor. The wood framing that you add to this rock-hard exoskeleton serves two purposes: First, it provides "chases" in which to hide wires, pipes and ductwork, and second, it creates a framework on which to hang drywall and/or paneling.

Your first task is to examine all existing wooden members in your basement. Carefully inspect wooden pilasters (posts), beams, rim joists, ceiling joists and sills for dry rot, fungus, insect colonies, water damage or structural defects. Keep in mind that rot spreads and that affected wood should be completely removed and replaced.

If you need support while you cut away damaged joists or do other overhead work, you can carry the load above by cutting a 2x6 or 4x4 to the right length and driving it into place where you need the support (see Fig. 14). You can also use screw jacks, which are metal pipes with a threaded post at one end. Set up plenty of bracing or props before you cut away anything, and if you remove a

section of any supporting member (a joist or beam, for example), use bolts to attach the replacement that you scab in its place. Also consider whether it is possible to leave some sort of permanent support (a post, for instance) directly under the repair.

Note: If you replace or even just double up an existing floor joist, run a bead of construction adhesive along the *top edge* (or narrow side) of the new board so it will be affixed to the flooring above and will not squeak.

Problems such as carpenter ants or termites should be dealt with by a professional exterminator and solved before you continue with other changes; don't just hide them away. Decide what mechanical details (pipes, wiring, ducts) will need repair or replacement. And check a final time to ensure that no water is seeping into the basement from cracks, holes or porous masonry and that none of the existing plumbing is leaking into the basement.

Because the rim joists sit above the masonry, this is also the best time to insulate them, although you may wish to wait until the changes in your mechanical systems (if any) are in their final stages of completion before you start stuffing insulation between the joists. To insulate, fill the joist spaces with fiber batts. Along walls that run parallel to the joists, fill the entire space between the rim and the next joist. On the other walls, fill the space between joists entirely and out from the wall a foot or so (see Fig. 15). You can also place insulation in the remaining joist spaces to provide sound abatement between floors.

Just as you did with the ceiling, take lots

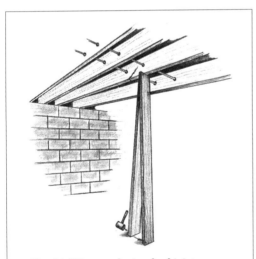

Fig. 14: When replacing bad joists, take the bearing load off the damaged member with a temporary brace.

of photographs before you begin to frame, to jog your memory later if necessary. Once everything is buried under drywall or paneling, it will be difficult to locate all those wires and pipes and ducts that once sat out in the open. Write important measurements directly on the concrete walls so that they will show up in the photograph. Chalk works well on dark walls, and a carpenter's crayon shows up on light walls, especially if they have been painted.

• T H E   B A S I C   W A L L •

UNLIKE MANY THINGS IN LIFE, A WALL is the sum of its parts, neither more nor less. To build a wall, you'll need to know the names of those parts, so that you won't have a senseless conversation going in your head, baffling you and annoying anyone to whom you speak: "Let's see, that thing nails to those things and both of them are nailed to the top things and the bottom thing." It sounds unprofessional and sloppy—a bad start if you want your wall to be well-constructed and solid. To build anything properly, you have to know what the pieces are called; after assembly, you can just go back to calling it a wall again.

Look on what follows as a refresher course and a bit of a test. If you understand the terms and the ways they are used, you are ready to soldier on. If, on the other hand, you are mystified by the nomenclature, stop, go find yourself a book on framing (one with lots

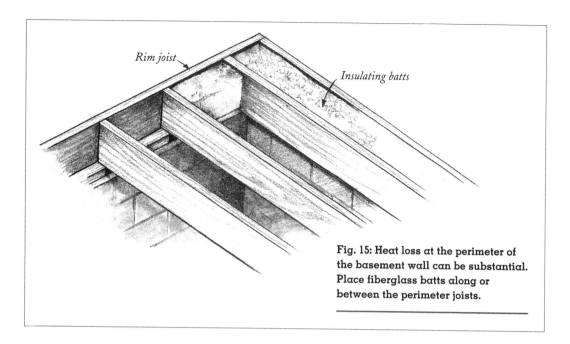

Rim joist

Insulating batts

Fig. 15: Heat loss at the perimeter of the basement wall can be substantial. Place fiberglass batts along or between the perimeter joists.

of diagrams) and give it a good going over.

Let us begin with the 2x4 or 2x6 "plates," which is the unlikely term for the topmost and bottommost parts of a wall, the horizontal wooden members that touch the floor and ceiling joists. The bottom plate, sometimes called the sole plate, makes contact with the concrete floor; for this reason, it should be made from treated lumber. At the top of the wall you will find, naturally, the top plate and, above that, the cap plate, which is sometimes also called the double top plate. The cap plate's prime function is to provide a means to connect intersecting walls; the top plate will be a long and continuous piece, and if it is spliced (as is the case with very long walls), it will be spliced over a stud. The cap plate, however, will be interrupted anywhere that walls intersect at right angles: The cap plate of the intersecting wall will lap over the top plate of the main wall, to tie them together

(see Fig. 16). Incidentally, the cap plate helps to strengthen the top plate, especially when the top plate is spliced.

Stud walls are named for the full-length vertical members of the wall, usually 2x4 or 2x6 boards. On an 8-foot-high wall, the studs will be 91⅝ inches long. Adding in the thickness of the bottom, top and cap plates, 4½ inches, gives us 96⅛ inches, or ⅛ inch longer than 8 feet. That extra ⅛ inch allows room for two sheets of 4-foot drywall, plus a bit more to compensate for irregularities in the concrete slab. Of course, in a basement, the full height of the walls will be determined by the floor overhead. A wall with no openings will have only studs and plates.

Any opening in a wall—a door or a window or a pass-through—means that there are studs missing, and that some other means must be provided to support the weight above. Across the top of openings, therefore,

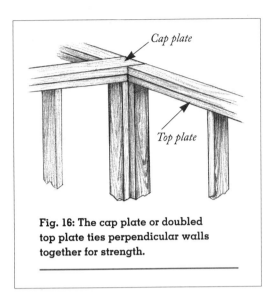

Fig. 16: The cap plate or doubled top plate ties perpendicular walls together for strength.

beams called lintels are installed. You may also hear these same members called "headers," a more generic term for any framing member that transfers or distributes a load or spans any opening.

Headers that do not support any weight are called nonbearing and are usually just a flat 2x4 or 2x6 placed at the height of, say, a door opening (see Fig. 17). A bearing lintel is usually built up, made from 2x8s or 2x10s or 2x12s (depending on the width of the opening and the live weight of the floor above). A "sandwich" of ½-inch plywood (the filling) and 2-by stock on both sides (the bread) makes a built-up beam that is 3½ inches wide, the same width as the studs and plates (see Fig. 18).

In many instances, these lintels can be placed tight against the top plate. But when you want the top of the rough opening to be a little bit lower, you will have to put cripples between the header and the top plate. A cripple refers to studs that are spaced on the same 16-inch layout pattern as the rest of the wall but are not full length: They do not touch both the bottom plate and the top plate. The short studs under a windowsill are also called cripples (see Fig. 19).

Trimmers, sometimes called jack studs or trim studs, are also not quite full length. They go directly under both ends of the lintel to support it. Depending on the weight to be supported, trimmers can be doubled for extra strength.

King studs refers to the full-length studs that nail to both ends of the header. The trimmers are also nailed to the king studs, creating a strong member that supports a header. **Note:** When trimmers are doubled, nail the king stud and first trimmer together *before* inserting and nailing off the second trimmer.

One last built-up member is called the channel, named because it looks like a channel when you put it on the floor. Basically, a channel consists of two studs placed parallel to one another with a third stud laid flat between them, and the whole assembly nailed together as well as nailed at the top and bottom plate (see Fig. 20). A channel provides a nailing surface for intersecting walls, as well as a neat corner of wood on both sides, essential for nailing drywall. Where two walls intersect, a channel must be placed in the main wall so that the end stud of the intersecting wall will have something to nail to. A channel should be placed directly under the spot where the cap plate is broken to accommodate an intersecting wall.

Got all that? Actually, framing is quite

simple. Here are some things to keep in mind to ensure that you do a good job:

•Weight must always be supported by wood (a lintel, for example, must always have a trimmer beneath it and not just be hanging from some nails).

•There must always be a surface to which drywall can be attached. In corners, you'll need to provide those surfaces.

•Always cut your framing members a slim fraction of an inch shorter than you need (maybe the width of a power saw blade, ⅛ inch, and even less than that for studs).

•Sink the heads of nails right into the framing material, not just flush; always hit the nail "one more time."

•Use your level often and carefully so that everything is kept level and plumb at every step of the operation. Repeat: At *every* step of the operation.

Now consult your drawings. A plan, in the sense of a detailed architectural and/or mechanical drawing (a floor plan), does not limit or confine your choices. Nothing is set in rock, so to speak, until after you nail on the drywall. But a floor plan provides dimensions, room measurements for floor coverings, a way to determine how much of each material you'll need, and a reminder that you are not just building haphazardly but to a purpose. In addition, a floor plan is necessary in most cases to obtain a permit from the local building department (although some do not require more than a general sketch showing proposed changes and details). If you deviate from your plan during the building phase, you should note each

Fig. 17: This nonbearing header in a partition wall forms the opening for a door.

change directly on the plan, as well as the date of the change.

Try to visualize how each aspect of framing affects the operation that follows, and begin your preparatory work, taking extra care to install all the backerboards you'll need. What are backerboards? Suppose the end of a bearing wall that you plan to install will terminate *between* two joists: How can you nail the ceiling drywall? For that matter, what will hold the top plate in place on a partition that is parallel to the joists? The answer to both questions is backerboards (sometimes called nailers) made of scrap lumber (see Fig. 21). Everything that you attach to the ceiling of your new basement space, be it wood or drywall, must be nailed or screwed to something solid, and in all those situations where the existing joists aren't enough, you have to add the backerboards before proceeding. And no matter where else you need them, you must install backerboards to the outermost ceiling joists, the ones running parallel to a wall (see

Fig. 22). You cannot have a gap all along the side of the room or at least part of your ceiling will fall down. These outer backers will provide a base to which to attach the ends of the ceiling drywall, and in some cases will be necessary to support the wooden frame that you'll need to support wall covering. (See page 49, "Furring the Walls," for further details about this.)

In some cases, you may be able to affix backers to the nearest joist by nailing through the sides of the joist; in other places, lacking room to swing a hammer, you may have to use

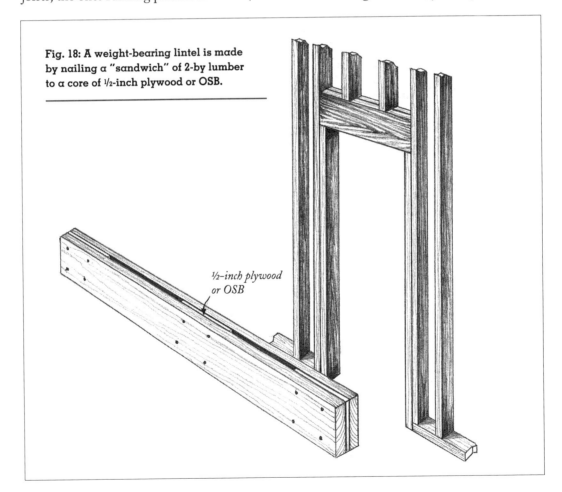

Fig. 18: A weight-bearing lintel is made by nailing a "sandwich" of 2-by lumber to a core of ½-inch plywood or OSB.

½-inch plywood or OSB

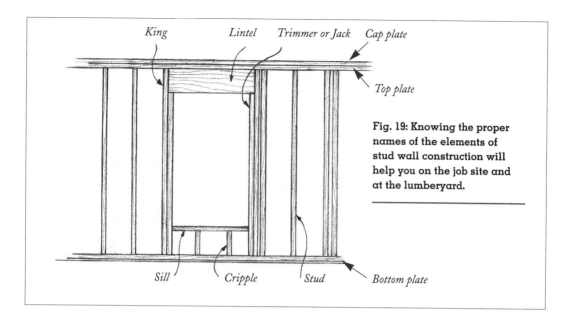

King   Lintel   Trimmer or Jack   Cap plate

Top plate

Fig. 19: Knowing the proper names of the elements of stud wall construction will help you on the job site and at the lumberyard.

Sill   Cripple   Stud   Bottom plate

construction adhesive and screws to secure them. All backers must be flush along the same plane as the ceiling joists. Do not underestimate the need to get framing members lined up perfectly: Once a sheet of drywall goes on, if there are even slight alignment problems, they will show up as long shallow mounds and dips in the finished surface. Check for planar alignment with a long straightedge that touches *at least* three joists at once.

· FURRING THE WALLS ·

IF YOU HAVE DECIDED TO SIMPLY PAINT your masonry or block walls, skip this next part, but remember that while painting the outside walls will save you a lot of time, you will have no insulation in those

walls and no place to put extra electrical outlets. The finished look will be decidedly institutional, plus you'll miss out on all the fun of putting up framing and drywall.

In most cases, basement walls are slightly uneven. If they are wavy, bowed or severely ugly, you can construct 2x4 walls all around the perimeter to correct the problem, but it is far less expensive to install furring strips (2x2s) directly against the concrete wall. If the walls were conscientiously constructed and are true and plumb, then strips are the way to go. This technique provides spaces for insulation such as foam panels, chases for wiring and pockets for electrical outlets; it also creates the wooden framework upon which to nail sheets of gypsum board.

To affix the furring strips (or "strapping," as the pieces are sometimes called), you may use any of a number of kinds of fasteners, each with its advantages and drawbacks. Hardened steel nails are fluted along the

Fig. 20: To tie walls and partitions together, make a channel with one flat face. This built-up member also provides edge nailers for drywall or paneling.

shank (see Fig. 23) and work best on concrete that has not cured for a long time, although even on older concrete you may obtain good results by drilling pilot holes at least half the length of the nail. You will need a heavy hammer and a strong arm to drive them. (They have a nasty habit of snapping sometimes when you hammer them, so be sure to wear eye protection or even a helmet-mounted full-face plastic shield.)

Lead or plastic anchors with screws are another option. First, drill marker holes through the furring strip, then drill into the concrete wall at the drill dimples, using a carbide drill bit designed for cement and concrete. Shove the anchors into place and screw into them. Although time-consuming to put in, these fasteners are very strong, as are the various proprietary screws now available that require no anchor and can be screwed directly into a pilot hole in the block or concrete.

Construction adhesive is another choice,

although in most cases it must be augmented with other fasteners. The adhesive comes in tubes and is applied with any ordinary caulking gun.

Finally, you may secure the furring strips with special nails driven by a powder-actuated gun, such as the Hilti. This system uses .22-caliber blanks to force a hardened nail through the furring strip into the concrete. It's by far the fastest and most reliable method, as well as the most potentially dangerous. Rental outlets carry these "guns" and can supply both the nails in various lengths and the cartridges. The nail is placed in the end of the barrel, a cartridge is inserted in the firing chamber and a sharp blow on the driver with a hammer triggers the charge. Make sure you place the nail in the center of the furring strip; if you find that the wood splits, you may have to drill small pilot holes.

You don't need a permit to shoot nails into your basement floor and walls, but take great care. Wear hearing and eye protection at all times, and keep your hands well away from the barrel. Seriously, these tools are loud, powerful and dangerous, and you definitely don't want to shoot yourself through the palm with a nail.

A final warning about leakage: If there is any possibility that moisture could wick through the basement walls, you must provide a barrier of polyethylene or tar paper between the concrete and the wooden strips you are about to mount. Check with your building inspector: In some localities you are required to include this precaution whether you think you need it or not. In some areas the

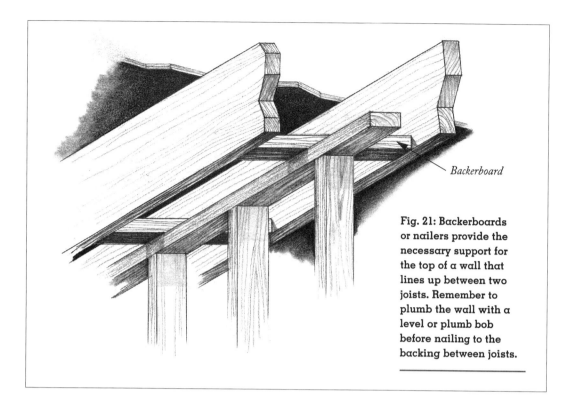

Backerboard

Fig. 21: Backerboards or nailers provide the necessary support for the top of a wall that lines up between two joists. Remember to plumb the wall with a level or plumb bob before nailing to the backing between joists.

code also requires a minimum amount of insulation in finished basement walls, so you may need to use deeper furring strips in order to accommodate the specified amount of fiberglass or rigid foam. In cold regions such as Ontario, Canada, for example, you need a moisture barrier *and* 3½ inches of fiberglass in order to achieve the required R-12 insulation. The simplest way to do this is to hold the poly or tar paper in place using one set of 1-inch furring strips set horizontally, and to then install an additional frame of 2x3s over that in order to enclose the insulation and to hold the drywall. Even if you have no such local requirements, however, take special care setting up the furring strips.

Note: If yours is a new house with a poured foundation, you should allow at least six months for that mass of concrete to completely cure and dry out before you seal it away behind a moisture barrier. If it is not allowed to dry, there is a risk of damage to the foundation, and that moisture will also make its way into insulation and framing members.

And now a final warning about *condensation:* Usually—that is, in walls that are above ground—insulation needs to be protected from the moisture that comes from *inside* the house. For people who haven't thought about this matter, this seems backward. After all, the wet comes from outside; that's why such care is taken with the roof and so on. But in any area that experiences winter freezing, the major water damage threat is not rainwater or leakage, it is condensation.

The air inside a house picks up moisture

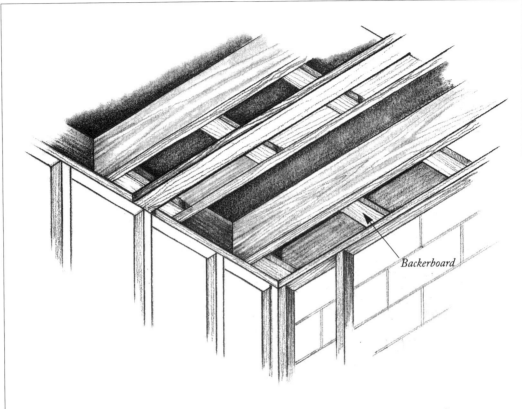

Backerboard

Fig. 22: Backerboards *must* be installed at the perimeter edge so you'll have something to which you can nail the drywall.

from everywhere, from clothes drying on a rack, from cooking, from steaming bathwater and showers, from plants and even from the human bodies perspiring and breathing. When that air comes in contact with a cold surface, the moisture condenses, and during the winter months, the most obvious cold surface is the inside of exterior walls. The drywall is warm, the insulation is warm, the studs and plates may even be warm, but the inside surface of the plywood sheathing will be at the same temperature as the air outside. If the indoor air gets to the plywood sheath-

ing, the moisture it contains will condense and soak the wood. And wood that gets wet on a regular basis begins to rot. The fiberglass insulation will also get wet and thereby lose its ability to trap heat (solid foam insulation is less vulnerable).

Because of the threat of condensation, most building codes now require an air-vapor barrier on the *warm* side of the insulation in a wall. That means that once a wall is built and once the insulation is installed, a continuous—uninterrupted, unpunctured—sheet of polyethylene must be sealed in place.

The plastic prevents condensation because it contains the indoor air and never allows it to reach a cold outer surface. Exterior walls in a basement should be provided with this continuous air-vapor barrier in just the same way as are the walls on the floors above. Keep in mind that you are going to have to install this polyethylene when you are making decisions about how and where to mount your framing.

That said (and duly considered by you), you can begin furring. Start with the top furring strip. Generally, this piece can be nailed directly to the joists or backerboards overhead. (If the basement wall is not plumb, you may have to come out a little on the top or bottom furring strip to compensate. But don't come out too much or you'll have to shim each furring strip with a shingle behind it. Check for proper position with a plumb bob or level. And make all the decisions about shim placements before you start firing off powder-actuated fasteners or driving concrete nails.) Now place the bottom furring strip. If the slab does not meet the wall cleanly at the bottom, you can cut a bevel on the back/bottom corner of the furring strip to make it fit flush against the wall and floor (see Fig. 24). Add the vertical strips next.

The layout of the vertical furring strips is critical: Think of them as studs for nailing 4x8 sheets of drywall. If you begin drywalling at the corner of the room, the edge of the drywall board must end in the middle of a furring strip, right? Place your tape measure at the corner and measure 15¼ inches (for 16-inch on-center spacing)—see Fig. 25—or 23¼ inches (for 24-inch on-center spacing). Drive a small nail at that point, hook your tape measure on it and continue your layout on 16-inch or 24-inch centers. This ensures that the first drywall sheet will bisect the fourth furring strip (or third, if your studs are on 2-foot centers), and each subsequent sheet will also reach to the middle of a furring strip.

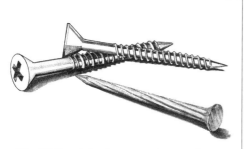

Fig. 23: Specialty fasteners for attaching furring strips include bugle-headed drywall screws and hardened-steel fluted concrete nails.

• WALL PLACEMENT •

THERE ARE THREE KINDS OF BASEMENT walls: (a) the outside walls, which we've already discussed; (b) bearing walls, which are any walls placed directly under the length of a beam or any walls perpendicular to the direction of the joists; and (c) interior partitions, which are walls that run parallel to the joists and basically act as room dividers.

One crucial difference between a bearing wall and a partition is that any openings in bearing walls will require lintels, built-in beams that will support the weight from above by transferring the load forces down through the trimmers, which are those studs into which you nail door jambs (see page 48, Fig. 18). Openings in partitions require only a light framework at the top of the opening to hold the drywall or paneling and to bring the wall down to door height (see page 47, Fig. 17).

Building frame walls in a basement is different from building frame walls in new construction. In new construction, you can always nail together an entire wall while everything is laying flat on the deck and then tip it up into a vertical position. If you try that in a basement, you will discover that the ceiling prevents you from raising the wall: It's like trying to put up walls with the roof already in place. The only way to build a bearing wall or partition in your basement is to set either the bottom plate or top plate first and use a plumb bob to determine the location of the other. Sometimes there is a way around this problem—we'll get to that in a minute—but first you want to be clear about the basic, slow-going, fail-safe technique.

Whether you place partitions going by locations on the ceiling (as when, for instance, you are avoiding ductwork soffiting or stairway framing) or whether you decide to begin at the slab and let the top plate end up wherever it will, you must use a plumb bob (see Fig. 26). For example, once you have installed the top plate, the next thing you do is drop a plumb bob down at each end and mark those locations on the floor. You then use those marks as your guides and connect them by snapping a chalk line. That line tells you where the bottom plate will be. Conversely, if you have already set the bottom plate, hold the plumb bob on the backer so that it lines up directly overhead, again at both ends, and snap a line along the ceiling joists to mark the location of the top plate. Top and bottom plates must be precisely plumb with each other or the wall will tilt. Even worse, if the top and bottom plates are plumb at one end but not at the other, your wall will have a giant twist in it, which makes a good drywalling

Backerboard

Damp proofing from ground to basement floor on inside of wall

Bevel cut on furring strip

Fig. 24: Furring strips provide a nailing surface and an insulatable air space.

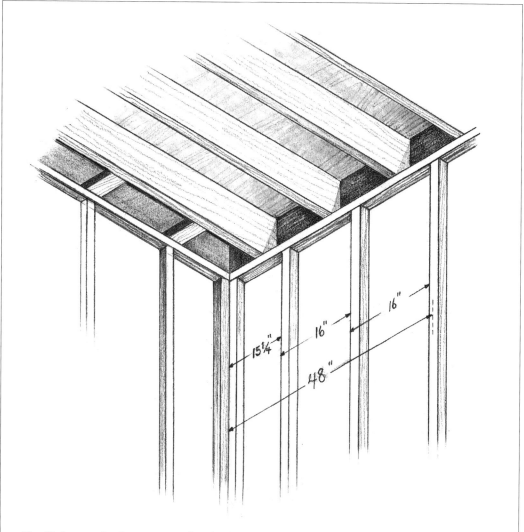

Fig. 25: Lay out furring strips so that the first one from the wall is at 15¼ inches; this way, the edge of an 8-foot drywall panel will line up at the center of a furring strip.

job impossible and door frames a bit tricky to get right.

The bottom plate can be secured directly to the slab by means of expansion bolts, lead or plastic anchors, bolts set in the slab with hydraulic cement or epoxy, steel nails, construction adhesive or powder-actuated nails.

Nail the top plate either to the joists or, where needed, to backers nailed between joists. And remember, if your wall is a partition and running parallel to the joists above, you will have to install backers between two of those joists to catch the edges of drywall sheets; the backers will also serve to attach the top plate of the partition. (We know what you're thinking, but no, there's no way around the nuisance job of nailing in those spacers. Even if you deliberately place a partition directly beneath a joist, you must still install backers on both sides of the top plate, in order to attach the drywall.) Measure between the two joists under which your partition will run, then cut enough 2x4 or 2x6 backers to set at 2-foot intervals, including the ends (see page 51, Fig. 21).

Having set the top and bottom plates, you must now cut the studs. Begin at each end of a wall and measure up from the bottom plate; it helps to stand on a ladder or turtle (see Fig. 27) to read the tape accurately. Measure to within 1/16 inch; you'll want each stud to be tight between the top and bottom plates but not so tight that it lifts the floor joists. And measure each stud individually: There may be slight variations due to an uneven slab or, heaven forbid, uneven joists above.

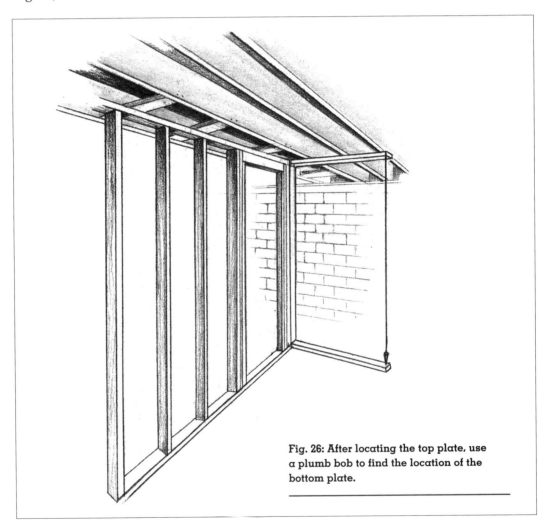

Fig. 26: After locating the top plate, use a plumb bob to find the location of the bottom plate.

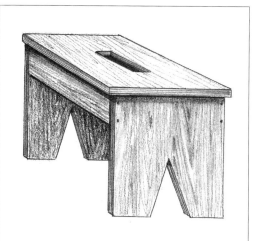

Fig. 27: A small bench, sometimes called a turtle, can provide enough elevation to work on projects above eye level.

Each stud will be held in place at top and bottom by toenailing four 2½-inch common or box nails (you may use galvanized nails if you like for extra holding power, but be prepared to pull out any benders with a set of nippers). Place the point of the nail about the thickness of your finger from the plate, and set it with a tap of your hammer. You may need to use a finish hammer for this job, because many framing hammers have too big a poll (face of the hammer) to drive toenails all the way. A finish hammer gives more control for nailing small nails anyway, and is a friendlier weight for driving nails overhead.

If you have difficulty toenailing—it takes practice—try reversing the nail and hitting the tip. This dulls the point so that it won't split the wood and provides a flat-bottomed dimple in the stud that will hold the point for you (see Fig. 28).

Occasionally, you may cut a stud slightly too short to fit snugly between the top and bottom plates. If this happens, measure the other stud locations to see whether that stud will fit better in another spot on the layout. If you find no place where it fits snugly, toenail the top end of the stud to the top plate, then slide a thin shim, such as a cedar shingle, between the bottom end of the stud and the bottom plate. You can then brace one side of the stud with your foot while you toenail the other side. If you nail the stud to the bottom plate first, the top end will wave about and fall over and generally make life difficult for anyone with only two hands.

And now for the "alternative" technique we promised. You can sometimes frame walls for a basement space just as you would in any other situation: building the wall sections flat on the floor and raising them into place all in one piece. However, you first must make certain that you will not be prevented from positioning the wall by a pipe or soffit or beam in the ceiling. Then you must build your wall sections a couple inches shorter than the full height of the ceiling overhead. You lift them into position by placing blocks beneath the bottom plate after these too-short sections are standing upright.

▪ S L E E P E R S ▪

IF YOU PLAN TO USE VINYL OR CERAMIC tile on the floor, skip this part. But if you want wood floors or wall-to-wall carpet, or if you like the idea of warm, insulated basement floors under your feet, you may wish to lay down sleepers. Sleepers are basically a wooden framework of 2x4s affixed to the concrete slab, eventually sheathed with ¾-inch tongue-and-groove (T&G) plywood or similar decking. (One final inducement: Concrete floors can cause foot problems if you stand on them for any length of time.)

To secure the sleepers to the floor, you can use any of the methods described earlier for attaching furring strips. But the strips *must* be firmly and permanently attached. Fill any voids under the sleepers with mortar or patching compound, or shim them with shingles. By placing the 2x4s flat instead of on edge, you will lower the floor by just over 2

inches; this will allow a little more headroom in the basement, and may obviate other problems such as raising the floor above the height of the sills on doorways leading outside.

Begin by laying a vapor barrier on the slab. This can be 6-mil plastic sheeting, 20-pound felt (sealed at the seams with asphalt) or an impermeable paint-on rubberized membrane. (Check your local codes for variant requirements on vapor barriers.) The goal is to prevent ground moisture from seeping up to the underside of your sheeting and causing rot or fungus problems, funny smells, or other basement woes.

Start with a perimeter band of sleepers, then space the intermediate sleepers either 16

Fig. 28: To start toenails, reverse a nail and strike it to produce a shallow dimple in the wood.

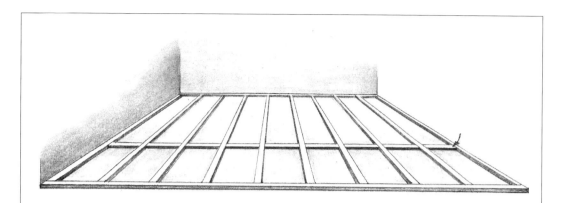

Fig. 29: Intermediate sleepers support the ends of plywood sheets in this sleeper system.

inches on-center or 24 inches on-center (we suggest 16 inches on-center since, unlike with the walls, you'll be walking around on the floor and want sturdiness). In either case, make sure that the ends of each tongue-and-groove plywood sheet will bisect a sleeper. If the sleepers run the length of the room, the sheets should run across the room. For a rock-solid floor, you can install intermediate sleepers every 4 feet so there is no possibility of a problem at the joint between any two sheets of plywood (see Fig. 29). It's not a bad idea to overbuild, because you don't want any flexion or bounce in the finished floor.

Secure the plywood sheathing with screws or ring-shank or screw-shank nails, augmented by beads of construction adhesive (just a thin bead everywhere the plywood touches; you don't want it squeezing up messily through the joints). If you are in the mood to be really clever, you can arrange your sleepers so that they are lined up with the studs in the wall. That way, after the drywall is on and finished and covered with a primer coat of paint but before the finish floor is in place, you will be able to locate studs in two of the four walls by sighting along the nailing lines in the floor.

A COOL, DARK PLACE FOR WINE AND VEGETABLES

·

*The Modern Root Cellar
Made Simple*

AROOT CELLAR IS A COOL, DAMP ROOM IN YOUR warm, dry basement that saves you energy by providing cheap refrigeration. A root cellar actually takes advantage of the otherwise unpleasant conditions of an underground space. If you are struggling to seal away moisture and trap in the heat so that you will have more useful space downstairs, perhaps you want to take a path of less resistance and set aside at least some of that area for food storage.

The dirt-floored cellars in old houses, while a horror for heat loss and moisture and soil gas incursion, were very effective for cold storage. Even houses built on piers often had a dirty hole dug under them that one entered through those familiar sloping doors. The house shaded a cellar from sunlight. The earth resisted tem-

perature swings, allowing the cellar to neither freeze nor get too hot. There were no windows, so no light with its destructive ultraviolet rays. The door provided periodic ventilation, and moisture from the dirt floor kept things from drying out. It was an entirely passive system that worked very well, and it can be reproduced in a modern basement.

The first thing to do is reverse your thinking about insulation for a moment. You don't want to trap heat in a root cellar; instead, you want to isolate an area from the rest of the house and leave it out in the cold. If your house is older and has an outside stairwell to the basement—the kind with the sloping cellar doors—you can use that area as a root cellar with little or no modification. If there is no door at the bottom of the stairs, you'll need to install an insulated one. (Actually, this is a good idea whether or not you want a root cellar.) You can do this in a couple of ways. One is to attach a slab of rigid foam insulation to a solid-core door you purchase at a building supply center or scrounge at the demolition yard; use four long bolts and large washers in addition to an adhesive. The second is to frame the door itself from 2x2s or 2x4s, then insulate it with fiberglass batts (see Fig. 30) sandwiched between layers of plastic. Cover the outside with plywood or paneling or even drywall, and leave the inside with just the layer of plastic so that weight is kept to a minimum. Hang it with oversized hinges, the kind you find at farming supply stores or big hardware supply depots. You also want a latch that keeps the door closed tight.

Once the door is in place, you can experiment with a thermometer to discover what temperatures you get in this space during different seasons. You'll find that the temperature varies at different steps. You may have to insulate the upper doors as well if things heat up too much in the summer. Through the cold months of the year you will be able to regulate the temperature by opening and closing the lower door.

In newer houses, including many basic tract bungalows, the cast-concrete front porch sits atop a full foundation wall. In many cases that enclosed space is connected to the rest of the basement by a proper door. (If you have such an arrangement, you probably already use the space as a junk closet.) While it can make for damp storage, especially if there is no floor poured in that area, it can be an excellent root cellar with the addition of a few shelves. Here, again, you may want to install an insulated door.

In other cases, the space under the porch is simply closed off. That's how it was in the house Tom grew up in. When his dad was repairing salt damage to the steps and broke out a section of concrete, there it was, an amazing secret chamber, and it was in *their* house. He wanted his father to make him a hidden doorway, but that didn't happen. Tom knew it was there, however, and that was almost exciting enough. That same space may be there in your house, too, with block walls that go all the way down to footings at the same depth as the others under your basement walls. The builder simply didn't bother with a door and instead blocked it up.

If you have a front porch and do not have access to the space under it, you can investigate by first digging down right beside the outside of your porch to see if there is indeed a block foundation (there better be, or your porch is going to sink). If there is, go inside and break out a block near the top of the wall in the area where you'd put a door into this hidden space if it turns out you need one. Then stick a flashlight in there and have a look. It's possible you'll find a space that only extends down 4 feet or so to below the frost

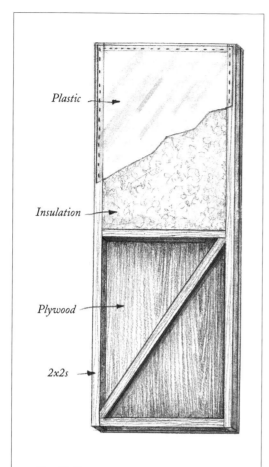

Plastic

Insulation

Plywood

2x2s

Fig. 30: You can construct an insulated door for a root cellar out of plywood, plastic, insulation and 2x2s or 2x4s.

line, but that's unlikely unless the porch was added after the house was built. You'll probably find a tiny room with walls directly below the edge of the porch. If that's the case and you want to create a root cellar, purchase a 3-foot section of 2x2 angle iron or a section of block lintel from the building supply center and use it to support the area over the door you cut out (see Fig. 31). You will have to chip out the mortar on either side of the

door opening so you can slip the angle into place, but a cold chisel can make short work of the job. Mortar the angle in place, then frame a 2x6 rough opening appropriate to the door you have available or plan to purchase.

▪ MAKING A CELLAR IN YOUR CELLAR ▪

IN OTHER NEWER HOUSES, ADDING A root cellar isn't quite as simple: You'll need to portion off part of the basement. Work in a corner if you can so that the ratio of cold wall (existing concrete, block or stone) to warm wall (the stud walls you build) is as high as possible, and pick an area that receives minimal sunlight. This means a northern corner unless you have a large veranda shading some other side of your house. Then frame in an area that you feel meets your needs, keeping in mind that a relatively small space will hold a lot of food. A full bushel basket, for instance, can sit on a shelf just 18 inches deep. Plan your little room so that shelves go against the cold walls.

Refer to the instructions on framing (see Chapter Four) and build stud walls to enclose the space. Include as much insulation as you have room for and as you can afford. This means building 2x6 walls if there is space available, and going with rigid foam insulation if you have to in order to achieve at least R-23. The ceiling will have to be insulated just as carefully as the walls so that your walk-in cooler doesn't chill the room above. And, again, the door to your root cellar will have to be insulated. The floor should remain bare concrete, and if it's a little damp, all the better.

As with any space you insulate, you will need to protect the insulation from moisture in the air, and that means a continuous air-vapor barrier. In this case, however, you'll need two. The air-vapor barrier always goes on the warm side of the insulation, which means that you need it on the living-space side of the root cellar wall. But because the enclosed cellar will be a relatively moist enclosure, it's best to protect the fiberglass batts on the inside surface as well. The ceiling will need the same treatment: Cover it with poly, running it up and around each joist, then install the batts and seal them in with a second layer of plastic.

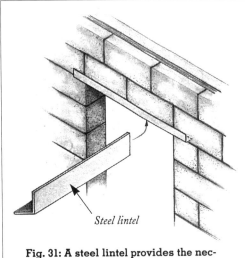

Steel lintel

Fig. 31: A steel lintel provides the necessary support above new openings in concrete foundation walls.

If you decide to go with rigid foam panels, rather than fiberglass batts, for insulating the walls, door and ceiling, the cost will be greater but you'll have less work to do. Seal the joints between panels, and in one step you will provide both temperature control and prevent the movement of air. Whereas you should probably put a finish wall over fiberglass and poly in order to protect against punctures, the rigid foam can be left exposed on the inside of the root cellar, which can help you save back a bit of the extra cost and a lot of time.

▪ V E N T I L A T I O N ▪

A ROOT CELLAR SPACE MUST ALSO BE ventilated, but only minimally. This can be done in a number of ways. If you have a window in a suitable location, one that you don't mind losing from the living space, build your room around it. Paint the glass black or cover it with opaque film—a root cellar should be dark—and leave the window open a crack. If the window opening admits an appreciable amount of light (if it's as bright as day in your root cellar, for instance), attach a series of wooden louvers to the outside of the window. You may want the window open all the time or you may have to close it during cold snaps, depending on how well insulated your root cellar is and on such other factors as the usual direction and strength of the wind in your area and the location of your cellar in relation to that wind. The same applies to small louvered

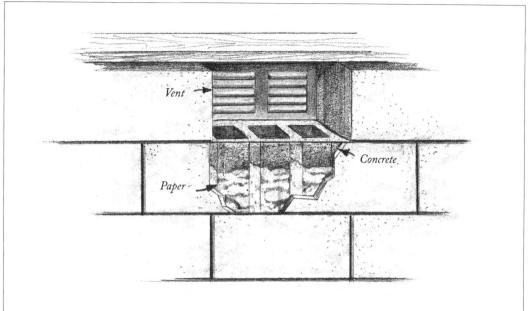

Fig. 32: Louvered metal vents can be retrofitted into a concrete block wall by removing one block.

metal vents that you can purchase and install in a block wall if you have no window available (see Fig. 32). Such units fit into openings the size of a standard block and are installed after you remove a single block from high on the wall.

To install the block vent, select a concrete block in the top course, just under the mudsill—the first wooden member you see—and in a location that won't be obstructed by items placed on an adjacent shelf. Now smash it out, using a brick hammer or small sledge. Keep in mind that the blocks are usually hollows with solid partitions; you want to aim for the hollow parts. Once you've broken through, you may need to clean up using a cold chisel to chip away all the old mortar (you can drop the smaller pieces down into the holes in the blocks below). Then with everything squared up, find something you can use to plug up those holes. Masons working on new walls use empty masonry bags—anything similar will do, even newspaper. Push it down into the holes so that only half of each of the two voids in the first block remains (see Fig. 32), then fill the remainder with ready-mix concrete (available at building supply centers), which requires only water.

UPSTAIRS, DOWNSTAIRS, INSIDE OUT

■

*Building Steps,
Doorways and Windows
from Scratch
and from the Catalog*

G O INTO ANY UNFINISHED BASEMENT, AND ON the way down you will discover that the stairs are steep and cheap—usually two open carriages with dadoed or cleated planks for treads and no riser boards. Count on it: This is going to be unsuitable for the high traffic into and out of the living space that will eventually be your finished basement.

Stair construction is by far the most difficult aspect of carpentry. Unless you are a fairly accomplished carpenter, comfortable with the higher mathematics involved and familiar with the myriad requirements of building codes that apply, and unless you are well-versed in the use of a framing square, dividers and stair gauges, it would be wise to hire a contractor with the right tools and experience to build your stairs, either *in situ* or as a job of millwork. Given the total rise (distance from basement floor to the top surface of the floor above) and run (total horizontal distance available for the steps), an expert can design and build a stair system off the site

that will fit perfectly. You can probably install it yourself to save money, and all you'll need for that is a pair of extra hands and another strong back to help lift it into place.

The hardest and most crucial part of stair building is the initial calculation phase. No two builders construct stairs the same way, but all well-made stairs will be virtually identical given the same stairwell, rise and run. Some carpenters use mathematics to figure out the stair dimensions, others use their squares as calculators, and still others will succeed with a trial-and-error method involving wing dividers. It wouldn't hurt to take your total rise and run to an expert and have someone who has built many stair systems do the actual calculations. You can also find general construction books in the library with tables that call out the exact unit rise and unit run for any given total rise and run. And there are entire books about building stairs that include tables for every imaginable stair system. Above all, you don't want to use the hold-and-mark method when cutting stair carriages, because it won't work, won't work, won't work.

■ TAKING
STOCK
OF STAIRS ■

To BEGIN, CHECK THE EXISTING STAIRcase for placement in your floor plan. Does your stairwell have plenty of elbow room, and is it situated where it won't interfere with proposed partitions? Are the stairs wide enough? (A typical width is 36 inches, but 38 inches to 40 inches is preferred. Check your local building codes for minimum stair width.) Do the stairs lead down into the room in a way that makes using them convenient? Is there at least 6½ feet of headroom, preferably 7 feet, where you pass under the edge of the stairway opening? If the answer to any of these is no, you may decide to remove the existing stairs, block off the old stairwell and rebuild your stair system in a more suitable location, such as in one corner of the basement where the run can be broken into two sections with a landing.

Another option is to leave the stairwell where it is, perhaps to be widened a few inches or even radically expanded for a circular staircase. This latter type of stair system is brutally complicated, stringently controlled by building codes and never recommended as an amateur project. However, if you find that no part of your basement is suitable for a standard inclined staircase, you might *have* to consider a circular stair system. They aren't cheap—prices range from $500 to $2,000, depending on options such as oak-faced treads and a funicular oak handrail—but this may be your only alternative.

Nationwide, there are a number of companies that will take your stairwell measurements and build circular stairways to your specifications. These companies advertise in such publications as *Fine Homebuilding,* and will send you brochures galore for the asking. You can handle the entire transaction by phone or letter—no salesperson will call. Jeff knows of one couple who took the measurements and sent a sketch of their basement layout to such a company. In less than a week, a truck brought several boxes with all the components, detailed instructions on how to assemble them and a list of tools they would need. They installed the staircase themselves in one afternoon, just as the brochure promised they could, and everything worked perfectly.

You might also consider having your staircase built locally if you live near a large urban area with shops that do custom millwork. One advantage is that a local company can recommend qualified installation experts in the area to put in your staircase with you hovering over them. If something goes wrong, they're close enough to put it right, either on the spot or back at the shop. A local firm can also provide the names of satisfied customers, some of whom may let you look at a real working circular stair system in their own homes.

In all likelihood, in order to modify the typical basement stairwell opening, you will have to move joists or bearing beams. This will be true whether the opening runs parallel or perpendicular to the joists (see Fig. 33). You may need a landing to reduce the angle of incline, as old basement stairs may have an angle as steep as 40 degrees. An angle between 33 degrees and 37 degrees is preferable and may be required by local codes. If there is to be a door at the top of the stairs, codes also require a landing long enough so that the open door does not protrude over the first step. (You don't want to sweep people

off the landing by opening the door just as they've reached the top of the stairs.) The landing itself should be at least as long as the stair is wide, but not longer than 4 feet unless there is a change in stair direction at the landing.

These parameters have evolved over the years, and in most cases have been incorporated into building codes that also strictly define the height and depth of steps. Such guidelines ensure that the stair system will be safe and easy to use, resulting in a comfortable feel that feet will naturally recognize from years of climbing other stairs built to approximately the same ratio of dimensions.

Assuming the stairwell is suitable but that you want to change the stairs, pause for one last moment and note that beyond the technical requirements of stair building there is also the practical matter that each stair and riser should be cut to within ⅛ inch of all the others. Consider the difficulties and time involved in doing this yourself, as well as the cost of hiring a contractor, and make your decision about how to proceed accordingly—and carefully.

If you *still* decide to carry on yourself, the next task is to determine the exact total rise and run and to then select three 2x12s that are 2 feet longer than the total run. These will be your stair carriages, also called bearing stringers. They carry the weight.

To finish the *sides* of the stairway, you will probably want a semihoused stair system; that is, one enclosed on both sides with 1x12 non-bearing stringers. (A fully housed stair carriage system has tapered grooves rabbeted

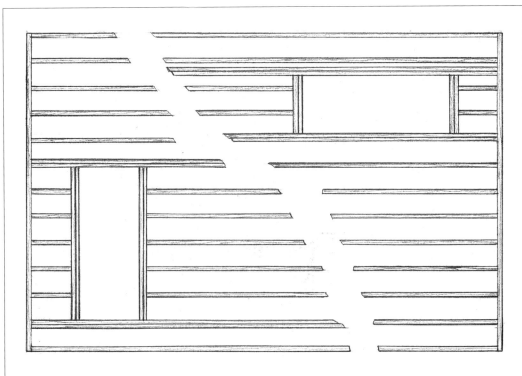

Fig. 33: Two stair openings, one parallel and one perpendicular to joist run direction. Note that the members adjacent to openings are doubled.

into heavy outside carriages, into which the risers and treads are set and glued. But this method is too hard—believe us, you don't want it.) Obtain two clear 1x12s (no knots, splits, checks or wane), also 2 feet longer than the total run, to serve as stringers that will enclose the sides. Put them aside for now. You will also need a couple of lengths of 2x4 to serve as the crosspieces that tie together the tops and bottoms of the carriages.

Now get a calculator and a piece of paper. Then, if you seriously intend to go forward from here and construct stairs for your basement, find yourself a good set of stair tables. Don't pass them up if they come bundled with a manual on stair building as well. The possible combinations of stair "lengths" (total run) and stair heights and angles of incline are practically limitless: Tables will show you more options than you could otherwise imagine. Two classic texts that are still making the rounds in used bookstores and libraries are *Stair Builders Handbook* by T.W. Love (1974; Craftsman Books Co., 542 Stevens Ave., Solana Beach, CA 92075) and *Audels Carpenters and Builders Guide #4* by Frank D. Graham (1945; Audel and Co., 49 W. 23rd St., New York, NY 10010). The former is a set of tables with some instruction; the latter is a book of detailed instruction.

You begin by finding the number of treads that you'll need. That's done by dividing the total rise by 7. The number of risers (the vertical aspect of the stairs, the bit in front of your toes when you are standing on a tread) will be one more than the number of treads, and every other dimension will be a variable function of these numbers.

Let's say the total rise is 8 feet. For an angle of incline just over 36 degrees, your calculations and your tables will tell you that you need, for example, 13 risers of 7⅜ inches each and 12 treads of 10⅛ inches each. The total run of the stairs will be 10 feet 1½ inches.

Set stair gauges (tiny clamps that tighten in place with a finger-tightened screw) on the framing square as follows: 7⅜ inches on the tongue (the short arm of the framing square) and 10⅛ inches on the blade (the long arm). Set one 2x12 carriage on a pair of sawhorses and place the square so as to mark the first step.

Beginning at the top, draw a line along the outside edge of the square to mark the riser, and another line along the outside edge to mark the tread. Move the square down into the next position and repeat (see Fig. 34). Finally, make the top vertical cut that will rest against the reinforced header at the top of the stair, then make the bottom horizontal cut where the carriage will meet the finished floor. Deduct the tread thickness from this last cut, and saw it off (again); this final cut adjusts the bottom riser height so that it matches all the others.

This is the point at which anyone but an expert stair builder begins to scratch the head and mutter; it is the reason amateur stair builders have so many difficulties. Think about the concept for a minute. You have made all your cuts as if the treads had an actual thickness of zero, but the typical tread is anywhere from 1⅛ inches to 1½ inches.

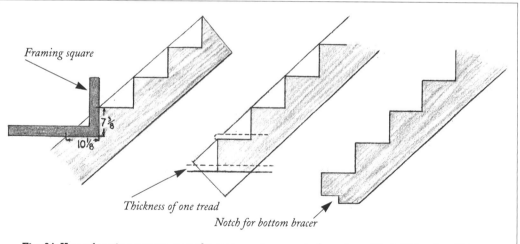

Framing square

7⅜

10⅛

Thickness of one tread

Notch for bottom bracer

Fig. 34: Use a framing square to make stair carriages out of good-quality 2x12 lumber. Note the two bottom cuts. The bottom riser is shortened by the thickness of a stair tread.

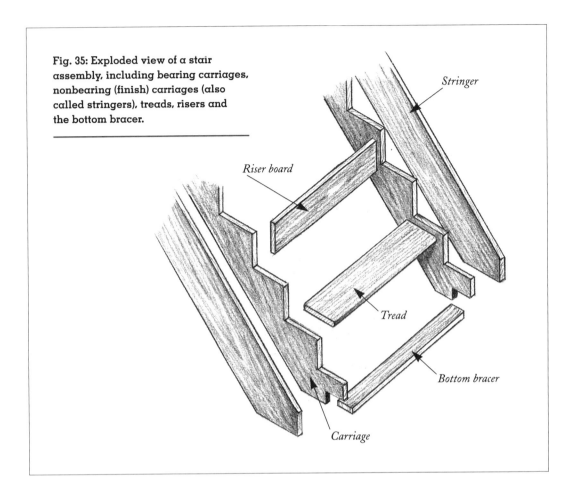

Fig. 35: Exploded view of a stair assembly, including bearing carriages, nonbearing (finish) carriages (also called stringers), treads, risers and the bottom bracer.

Stringer

Riser board

Tread

Bottom bracer

Carriage

Without this adjusting cut at the bottom, applying the first tread at the bottom would throw off all your individual riser heights, increasing them by the thickness of one tread all the way up to the landing. In theory, you can calculate the deduction before you begin cutting, but it is safer to make the bottom cut twice, in case you decide to change the thickness of the treads: Finished oak treads will be thinner than softwood treads intended to be carpeted. Follow this so far?

Cut notches, top and bottom, that will fit over the necessary crosspieces.

Check your first carriage by putting it in place and setting it perfectly at right angles (90 degrees) to the front edge of the landing. The top vertical cut should be a flush fit—no gaps—and the bottom horizontal cut should rest on the floor evenly along its length. All tread cuts should be level and the riser cuts plumb. If you have miscalculated, all you have ruined so far is one carriage board. If everything looks good, use your cut carriage as a template and mark out the other two load-bearing carriages, first one and then the other. Use a sharp pencil and/or a marking knife to make the layout: They must be exact duplicates of the first one.

Now lay one bearing carriage on one of the 1x12 nonbearing side stringers, with plenty of excess wood at both ends. Align the edges and make cuts at the top and bottom only (see Fig. 35). Repeat with the other 1x12. Careful now: These are expensive pieces of wood, and an error in cutting them will be glaringly obvious when the stairs are in place. Set these aside for the moment.

You have the option of setting each bearing carriage in place, one each at the outside and one up the middle, checking all measurements and nailing them to the crosspieces at the top and bottom, or assembling the entire carriage with treads and risers into a single unit and setting it in place as you would a stair system built and delivered as millwork. The first method is by far the easiest, especially if you're working alone. But proceed slowly: You should be checking all carriages with a level, square and straightedge as you go, ensuring that all treads are parallel and all risers are parallel. Don't forget to square the carriages to the opening, either. This is not something you want to eyeball unless you're fond of expensive disasters. Use at least a rafter square, and when you have the two outside carriages in place, measure their diagonals. The distance from the inside corner at the top of one carriage to the inside corner at the bottom of the other carriage should be identical to the other diagonal measurement.

How you attach the stair treads to the carriages is up to you, but countersunk screws are a good idea. Also, a little construction adhesive at all points of contact between treads and carriages and headers and risers is worth

the effort; if your stairs loosen up with use, the wafer-thin pads of adhesive will minimize squeaking.

Attach the 1x12 side stringers to the outside carriages with finish nails or adhesive, and your stairs are done. With everything in place and fastened, you now have "open risers"; that is, you can see through the gaps that separate each tread from the next one up. If you prefer a more finished look, you can close the gaps with boards cut to fit and nailed to the exposed surfaces of the supporting carriages with finish nails.

▪ D O O R W A Y S ▪

THERE ARE THREE KINDS OF ROUGH openings for doorways: one in a load-bearing interior wall, one in a nonbearing partition and one in an exterior (also load-bearing) wall.

For a load-bearing wall—an existing wall that crosses at right angles to the ceiling joists—you must frame in a lintel at the top of the opening for any door you install. The purpose of the lintel is to accept the weight that previously bore down on the wall itself and to transfer it to studs on either side of the new rough opening. The size of the lintel you have to build will depend on the width of the doorway you create. In general, a built-up lintel made of 2x8s turned on edge with a center "sandwich" of ½-inch plywood or oriented strand board (OSB) will be sufficient (see page 48, Fig. 18), although you may be required by your local building department to

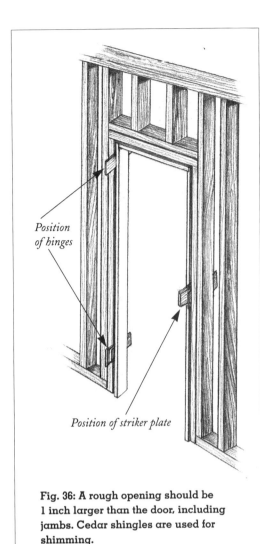

Position of hinges

Position of striker plate

Fig. 36: A rough opening should be 1 inch larger than the door, including jambs. Cedar shingles are used for shimming.

use 2x12s, especially if the doorway is under a beam or if the live load above is considerable—under a woodstove, for instance.

For a doorway in a partition wall—a wall that is not holding up the floor above but only dividing the space of the basement—you won't need a true lintel. Instead, a simple framework of 2x4s will suffice, with the short 2x4s set on the same 16-inch centers as all the others in the wall so that drywall or paneling will still line up properly (see page 47, Fig. 17).

Lintels, however, are essential for exterior doors. When adding a doorway to a finished basement, consult your building department to determine the proper size to use, and keep in mind that the lintel for a doorway leading outside may be holding up the entire weight of the house above it. The lintel for an exterior door is crucial if the opening is in a basement wall that supports the ends of the main floor's joists; that is, if the wall is perpendicular to the runs of the joists. If you are replacing a basement door with a better one of the same width, the existing rough opening may be sufficient, but if you are widening that doorway, plan on a beefier lintel.

When framing the rough opening of a doorway, careful measurement is critical. Before you can calculate the width of the rough opening that you will leave in the framed wall, you must know the total width of the door itself and its jamb, the light frame that fits around the door and within the rough opening, the wood to which the hinges attach. To that figure, add ½ inch of clearance on each side for shimming with cedar shingles (see Fig. 36). The top jamb will not be shimmed, so you can get away with up to an inch of clearance, but no less than ¼ inch. (The weight of the floor above in the living area is supported by the trimmers and studs, not the top jamb of a prehung door.)

Once you know the size of the rough opening, make your header 3 inches wider. The header fits between two full-length studs, but two more are fitted in right next to those studs. Installation of these trimmers will reduce the rough opening width to the correct dimension. Determine the location of your door and place the studs on either side as far apart as the length of the header. Make sure that the studs are the same distance apart at the top and bottom, and that both studs are dead-on plumb. Nail the header in place, nail trimmers to the studs on both sides and use a handsaw to cut out the bottom plate where it crosses the door opening.

Prehung doors will save time, which to some people's way of thinking is money. A prehung door can be placed in the rough

Fig. 37: Insert spacer shingles from both sides of the jamb: The two wedge shapes conform to each other and to the space between the jamb and rough opening for a snug fit.

opening, plumbed with a long level, shimmed at both side jambs and nailed in place—all in pretty short order. In the case of an exterior door, you then fasten everything in place by driving finish nails through the brick molding (that decorative lip on the exterior side of the frame) and through the jamb.

At the bottom of an exterior door unit is the sill, and you want to make sure you set it onto a healthy bed of caulking to avoid bug intrusion and air infiltration. Take the time to ensure that the sill fits flat and secure—that it cannot rock back and forth when walked on. Keep your caulking gun handy to seal up the edge of the brick molding when everything is in place.

Install the lockset and/or deadbolt, and you're done. If you're not familiar with how this is done, be sure to purchase a door with the holes for the lockset and/or deadbolt already drilled. Then it's just a matter of following the instructions for installing the hardware.

Hanging an interior prehung door is even simpler. Place it in the center of the rough opening and make sure the swing is correct. (Prehung doors are sold as either right-hand swing or left-hand swing.) Then align and plumb up the hinge side of the jamb first, using shingles thrust in from both sides of the jamb to adjust for plumb (see Fig. 37). The deeper you push the shingles, the further the jamb will be from the rough opening stud. Drive 2½-inch finish nails on either side of the door stop until ½ inch of the nail protrudes (you don't want to set them all the way yet, just in case you need to adjust the jamb further). **Note:** If possible, you want the shims set behind the door *hinges* on the one side and behind the *striker plate* of the door latch assembly on the other side (see Fig. 36). This may not always work out if the wood you're using for framing is twisted and uncooperative. (Someone may advise you to finish off your door installation by removing a couple of the hinge screws and driving longer replacements through the hinge plate and the door jamb, all the way into the solid framing member behind. While this probably isn't necessary for interior doors, it is a very good expedient when installing exterior doors. In either case, if you plan to take this extra precaution, you must ensure that the space behind the hinge plates is filled with shims. If you don't, that long screw you install will bite into the framing member and pull the jamb out of shape.)

Now adjust the top reveal (the distance from the top of the door to the bottom of the overhead jamb) so that it's level by moving the latch-side jamb up or down, then nail off that jamb, too. Drive the nails into the door stop and leave them protruding the same amount (½ inch) as on the other side. Does the door swing properly, with no sticking? Are all reveals good (is there an even, narrow gap all the way around the door)? If so, finish driving all the nails and set them with a nail set. At this point, you can still make minor adjustments with a flatbar between the rough opening and side jambs. Finally, score the shingles with a utility knife and snap them off flush. Now you're ready to apply casing (trim that surrounds the door) and install

the doorknob and striker. Open and close the door a few times: If it sticks anywhere, plane off the high spots.

· W I N D O W S ·

ONE OF THE OBVIOUS PROBLEMS WITH turning a basement into living space is the lack of natural light. Most basements have only a few windows, and those are generally small in size. If you want to avoid that closed-in bunker feel, you probably will need more windows, and you may want to increase the size of the existing ones.

At first glance, changing the windows in a basement looks like a major undertaking. In truth, there's probably less to it than to many of the jobs associated with your downstairs renovation, and the effects on your finished living space will be dramatic, guaranteed. For the price of a new unit and a couple days work, you can easily replace the little jail-cell hatches you have with something higher and wider and—most of all—brighter. Even windows that provide no view increase the perceived spaciousness of any room, and this certainly applies to basements.

When you are ordering windows, keep in mind that casements and awning-style windows project out from the house when opened. Avoid these styles, or at the very least measure your window well in advance to ensure that there is room for the operating units to swing. For most situations, you are probably best off with a simple slider.

If you plan to add windows and if some

of the new units will extend below grade, you will need to create a window well, a hole you dig so that your new window isn't blocked by dirt. You should give this hole some careful thought. On the one hand, the larger the hole, the more light you get. But the bigger the window well, the more likely it is to get in your way. Also, a big window well will catch more rainwater, be a greater hazard to small children, collect more wind-borne garbage and leaves and be more of a chore to build. So for starters, plan on something roughly 18 inches front to back. Dig it out, then decide for yourself whether that admits enough light and go from there.

Ideally, a window well should drain all the way to the footing, which means that you may need to sink a vertical length of perfo-

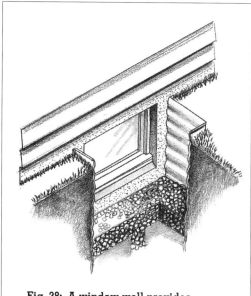

Fig. 38: A window well provides light where the basement wall is below grade level.

rated pipe from the bottom of the well to the gravel in which the drainage tile is buried at the base of the foundation. On the other hand, if the person who built the foundation did a good job, the area immediately surrounding your house should be backfilled with gravel. If so, any hole you dig will already drain readily, with the water making its own way to the footing.

The well itself should be wider than the window *and frame,* and should be deep enough so that after the bottom of the well is filled with a couple inches of ¾-inch crushed stone, it reaches a level 2 or 3 inches below the bottom edge of the window's wooden, vinyl or aluminum frame. You do not want there to be any possibility of water sitting in the window well and, even after a deluge, backing up so that it reaches the frame of the window.

To hold back the earth from your newly dug hole, you can purchase galvanized steel window wells (see Fig. 38) in a variety of sizes. You can also line the hole with stone, pressure-treated landscaping timbers cut to fit or even foundation-grade pressure-treated lumber and/or plywood. If you feel so inclined, you can even dig below the frost line, pour a footing and either lay up a small block wall or build forms and pour concrete to line the area. Keep the drainage material in the window wells clean: Clear away debris that blows in and even turn the gravel now and then to prevent weeds from getting any kind of hold.

To install a new window in a block wall or to install a larger window in an existing location, you will have to make a rough opening in the wall. This should be approximately an inch larger in both dimensions than the entire window unit. (Remember to allow an additional 3 inches in each direction for the window bucks, usually 2x8s or 2x10s, which form the wooden frame in which your basement window units must sit. Even if you are replacing windows with new units of the same size, you'll probably have to tear out the current bucks and replace them with new, treated wood.)

If you have never knocked a hole in a concrete block wall before, you will be surprised—and perhaps a little disconcerted—to discover how easy it is. First, you need to go outside and establish the exact location for the window. Keep in mind that the simplest way by far to deal with the block wall is to locate the top of the window opening directly under the mudsill (see Fig. 39), which means taking out the top row of blocks and however many more you need in order to create a large enough opening. To begin, use a cold

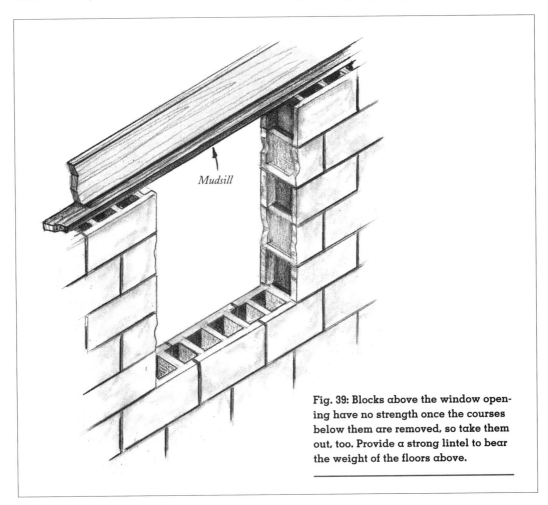

Mudsill

Fig. 39: Blocks above the window opening have no strength once the courses below them are removed, so take them out, too. Provide a strong lintel to bear the weight of the floors above.

chisel and hammer to crack the mortar all the way around the section of blocks you wish to remove. Do this inside and out, and make sure you are in the same spot on both sides of the wall by counting blocks over from some fixed point, such as another window or the corner of the house. Once that's done, depending on how delicate you want to be about it, you can either continue chipping away mortar until you free an entire block, then carry on to do the rest in the same manner, or you can spit on your palms before taking up the 8-pound sledge and blasting a hole right through with enough force to send bits of concrete block bouncing from your safety goggles—the ones you are wearing without fail, no matter which technique you chose.

By the way, if you want to smash it, hit a block about a quarter of the way in from the end; that's usually where it's hollow and weakest (see Fig. 40). Having suggested that, however, we should also warn you that, depending on local regulations and the soil conditions in your yard, some or all of the voids (as those hollows in blocks are called) may be filled with concrete, especially the ones in the top course, or row. There may also be an anchor bolt set in that concrete, a bolt that extends up through the wooden mudsill immediately above. These are used to secure the wooden structure to the foundation, but removing one of the bolts will not adversely affect your house. All you have to do is knock off all the concrete, then gently tap the bolt up and out of your way.

Concrete blocks are staggered in alternate courses, which means that in order to create vertical sides for your rough opening, you will need to cut blocks in half at every second row (see Fig. 39). You can rent various kinds of masonry-cutting saws and grinders to do this with, but it can also be done with the same cold chisel and hammer you used to begin making your opening. Simply use the chisel to score lines, inside and out, where you want the block to break, moving up and down and tapping gently. After a minute or so your patience will be rewarded with an even break. When you install the window, the mortar you use to fill in the gaps will tidy up the edges of the breaks and leave you with a professional-looking job (see Fig. 41).

If the height of the window does not fit within the hole made by removing full rows of blocks (as will happen if your blocks are roughly 8 inches per row and your window is 30 inches high), you can also cut the blocks horizontally, using a cold chisel and hammer. Or you can take the easier route and order windows custom-made to fit the opening. In most areas, custom window units can be purchased for about the same price as the ones you buy premade at large building supply centers.

A poured concrete foundation is much harder to work with than concrete block, but if you're willing to cut the concrete, you can make existing windows a little taller or wider. To do so, you'll need a masonry saw to cut the cured and reinforced concrete. Rental places sometimes carry these saws, but be advised, you *must* wear eye *and* ear protection: A flying chip of concrete can put out an eye very efficiently, and these saws make a racket like God tearing up the cosmic phone book.

Another possibility is to subcontract this work, which probably won't cost a whole lot more than you would spend to rent the tool (look under "Concrete Cutting" in the Yellow Pages). Whether you do it yourself or leave the job in the hands of a highly recommended professional, expect clouds of dust that are even worse than the mess from the drywalling project you took on last year.

Whether you are working with a block wall or with a poured concrete wall, once you have cut the hole, you must install the bucks and then the window unit itself. Be sure that the bucks are sealed to the foundation wall with the same care that an exterior door sill is sealed to the floor, and for the same reasons: so that no bugs will crawl in and no water will seep through. Fit the top and bottom bucks first, then install the sides in the space

between. The size of the bucks you need (2x6, 2x8 or 2x10) will depend on the thickness of the window unit you purchase, but be sure to use pressure-treated wood and be sure that the bottom buck either tilts slightly to the outside or has a beveled edge so that water runs off.

When you install the window unit itself, wedge it at the sides to hold it firmly in place, but do not jam it in tight top to bottom. Even if you fill the gaps at the sides and below the unit with mortar, you should not fill the top in tightly. A bit of space (½ inch) is necessary in case the mudsill and plate above the opening sag slightly. There won't be the same kind of movement builders expect in wood-framed walls, but you don't want even a tiny bit of shift to wedge the unit closed or possibly crack the glass.

And now a warning about the obvious:

Fig. 40: Break a concrete block at the weak points between internal walls or "webs."

Fig. 41: After removing the blocks, fill in all rough spots around the window opening with mortar to provide a solid bed for the window bucks.

If you are working in a foundation wall that holds up the ends of the floor joists above, you must provide a lintel above any window you install. The lintel above windows in the foundation are usually steel, but you can use wood if you prefer. Once again, there will be local requirements about the size of lintel required. Don't skimp on materials here: The weight of everything above is bearing down on the rim of the foundation (after all, that's what it's there for). If you simply want to replace old windows with new ones of the same size, do some research before you tear out the existing units. Be sure that the holes you have are a standard size for which you can purchase replacements at the local supplier, or that you have access to a retailer who can or-der custom-sized units to fit your needs.

Begin the job by removing the old windows. In many cases, the current basement windows will be aluminum-framed sliders or simple fixed windows with wooden frames and muntins. See if a local window contractor can provide a free estimate for windows, including cost of removal, and try to get the removal and installation labor on the bid as a separate expense. You may be able to take out the old windows and put in the new ones yourself, thereby saving in labor costs, which can be as much as 50% of the bill.

To remove old aluminum windows, take out the sliding section and set it in a safe place. If the fixed section can be removed easily, so much the better, but quite often it can't. Locate the points on the side and bottom where the flange is nailed. Slip the thin end of a flatbar under the flange and gently pry—but not too much or you may break the glass. Once the nail head is loose, reverse the flatbar and pull it out. Work carefully, and keep looking for nails that may be hidden under molding. It helps to have a second person holding the window from the inside so it won't fall out.

If you have wooden windows, the old rectangles whose six panes continually require new glazing, rejoice. You can usually remove the stops and pull them right out, although sometimes a nail or two will be driven into the wood part of the window to hold them in place. Be careful not to bend this kind of window when you're taking it out; the glass can shatter under stress, just like you.

A STRAIGHT FLUSH BEATS A FULL HOUSE

.

*Plumbing in the Basement
(or Defying the Law of Gravity)*

W HEN IN THE COURSE OF HUMAN EVENTS IT becomes necessary to reroute plumbing in one's basement, it isn't necessarily essential to call in a professional plumber. Amazing strides have been made in plumbing over the last 30 years, and among the most pleasant of these are rigid copper tubing and new types of plastic supply and drainage pipes. No longer is it necessary to plumb with steel pipe or to learn how to tamp oakum into the bell of a cast-iron waste pipe, and you no longer need the equipment and skills to melt and pour lead in on top of that oakum. With a little bit of research and a steady hand, even a 10-thumbed do-it-yourselfer can learn to plumb.

On the other hand, no one will call you a coward for enlisting the help of a local licensed plumber. For a reasonable fee—definitions of "reasonable" vary, depending on locale and plumber demand—this person will tell you what you need to do and how to go about doing it within the constraints of the code. You can even agree to do certain time-consuming (read "incredibly expensive") aspects of the job yourself, and leave the brain work and actual installation of fixtures to this expert.

Let's say you want to install a full bathroom in your finished basement: tub and shower combination, toilet and sink. Let's also say that you have tentatively established the proposed location of this new bathroom, and you have cleverly placed it as near as possible to the existing soil stack so that you can drain and vent your new tub, toilet and sink using this existing pipe. (We should take care not to seem too casual with this suggestion about locating your plumbing. Unless your new drains—toilet and sink and tub— are near the main stack, you will be required to provide venting for the drains, and that means running vent pipes all the way to the attic or even out through the roof.) Check your local codes to see how far a new fixture can be placed from an existing drain-waste-vent (or DWV, as plumbing contractors and inspectors call it). Finally, let's assume your plumbing skills are less than expert but greater than zero, and that you want to do as much of the work yourself as possible.

▪ TRACKING THE PIPES ▪

NOW WOULD BE A GOOD TIME TO find, amid the maze of pipes running under your living area, a hot water pipe and a cold water pipe. These pipes often run parallel throughout your house, and it's easy to tell which is which: The cold water supply is cold to the touch, and the hot water supply is hot enough to tell the difference with your bare hand. They may be steel or copper, but either way, you'll be able to tell which pipe is which. Trace them as far as you can in both directions. Keep track of these pipes, because you're going to be tapping off them to install fixtures that use clean hot and cold water at the supply end.

Most likely, the cold water from the street or from your private well enters the house through the basement; it does in 99% of houses with basements. Look for the main water shutoff valve, also called the gate valve—the valve you or the last plumber closed before fixing any major problems or broken pipes (see Fig. 42). Water supplies are usually ¾-inch or 1-inch pipes at the service entrance. Find that valve and pipe, and mark its location well: Take some Polaroids. Draw a diagram. (**Hint:** If you live in a city, there will be a meter squatting nearby through which the water runs.) That's where you'll "tee off" your cold water supply—insert a "T" connector that allows you to branch off with a new section of pipe—on the house side of the valve and meter.

Don't cut in on the wrong side of that valve, or you won't be able to pay all that you owe to the utility company, and you also won't be able to turn off your water for a broken pipe or any of the other emergencies that one always hopes won't come up. In fact, if you cut in on the wrong side of that valve, you will cause a flood that will stop only after you contact the municipal authorities and wait for their trucks to arrive.

Next, locate your water heater. Is it in the basement? Good. Most houses with basements have the water heater downstairs. If not, you can tee off the hot water supply pipe right in the closet where it now resides, then go straight down through the floor and voilà, you will have hot water heading toward your new downstairs bathroom.

Now, head for the DWV pipe, which is usually the biggest pipe in your basement: a large cast-iron thing on old houses and a large black ABS plastic thing in newer houses; maybe copper if a millionaire built your house or if it was ever used as a commercial building. That's the eventual destination of all your wastewater; at least it is if this pipe leads to a central city sewer system. If you live in the country and have a septic tank and graywater field with separate drainpipes, you'll have to isolate both pipes, because sewage will go in the first and bathwater in the second; codes vary on the type of waste that may be sent to the septic tank. Once again, check with your local building department for enlightenment. In fact, program your telephone with that number for easy one-touch dialing, because lots of codes apply to plumbing.

Plan the supply and DWV pipe layout

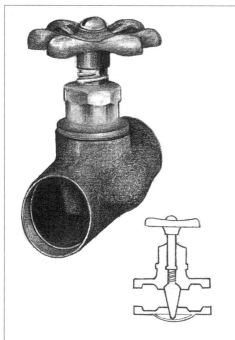

Fig. 42: The most important valve in your house is the gate valve, which shuts off all incoming water.

disaster if that pipe contains water under pressure and eventual disaster if the pipe only drains water every time the toilet flushes or the tub empties. Anyone who has done renovations, or new construction for that matter, has hit one of those protective metal plates with a drywall screw and thanked God for proper preparation. It happened to Tom two days ago.

If your drill isn't up to the job, buy one or rent a special offset drill like the plumbers use: It needs to make a perfectly straight hole. You'll probably need some sharp new bits as well, up to 2 inches, or you can purchase "hole saws" that look like serrated-edged cups attached to regular high-speed bits. Instead of drilling out a hole, hole saws cut out a circular plug. Either way, any money you spend on tools now will pay off very shortly.

The wall through which your plumbing supplies and wastes will run is called a wet wall, for the obvious reason. Since the waste pipe will be 1½ inches in diameter and the toilet vent a hefty 4 inches, and since you'll have to direct these pipes through the centers of the studs, you'll want this wall to be made of 2x6s (see Fig. 43). That will give you enough space to maneuver.

Do the waste line plumbing first; it's easier to run the smaller supply lines around the heavy plastic pipes than the other way round. Begin by plumbing the closet bend (that's the floor flange and trap for the toilet) and the DWV. Most toilet floor flanges should be 12 inches out from a wall, but check your toilet to be sure, and as you calculate that 12 inches be sure to allow for the thickness of drywall

to take the most direct route to your new bathroom. You'll need a good drill to make the holes through the central axis of the studs and joists. Remember, putting a hole—or, God forbid, a notch—anywhere else weakens the wooden members. When you feel you absolutely must make a notch in a joist, keep it near the end, never in the center of a span where it has the most tension. A notch in a stud should never be deeper than 2½ inches. Reinforce your cutout with steel strapping tape or, better yet, a steel plate afterward. When you've finished with all this plumbing and wiring, you're going to want to attach drywall to these same stud walls, and driving a drywall nail through a pipe means instant

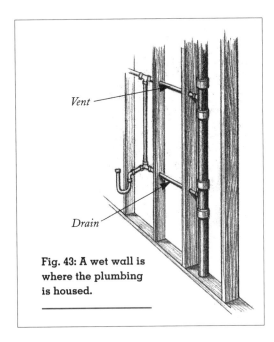

Fig. 43: A wet wall is where the plumbing is housed.

and any other structure that you plan to install later, such as a set of shelves behind the toilet. This is the point where you'll want to ask your pet plumber to check your work or diagram: Poorly vented fixtures don't work worth a hoot. Add vent branches to the main stack as you need them, and if you must install another large vent, make sure that it can be hidden inside the walls in the living space above your new bathroom. If you don't plan the placement of such pipes carefully, you'll end up with a conversation piece, a big homely pipe running up from the floor in front of your couch. Explanations won't help, nor will they be necessary. Everyone will know what you did.

In plumbing the waste lines, you'll probably be working with existing cast iron and with ABS. Your plumber or building inspector will tell you about neoprene seals and clamps, such as the Tie-Seal, or an MJ (me-

chanical joint) clamp, which can be used to connect new ABS to existing cast-iron pipe, and surely someone will mention cutting cast iron with a hacksaw. Prepare to sweat. It's virtually impossible to cut through cast iron with anything short of a military laser, but you can score a line 1/16 inch deep with a hacksaw and rap all around the score with a hammer. Some people have gotten good results with a diamond-encrusted wire blade, which will score a little deeper. Far better, ask your local rental outlet or plumbing supply center for a cast-iron pipe cutter. This daunting gadget consists of a 4-foot handle with a length of oversized bicycle chain hanging from one end (see Fig. 44, top). There are cutting wheels incorporated into the links, and the loose end of the chain is passed around the iron pipe and attached to hooks on the handle. To operate the cutter, you tighten the chain by rotating or cranking the handle. The tension mounts, and before you know it—certainly before you expect it—there comes a loud snapping bang and you find the pipe is cut neatly across. It is the purest tool magic.

With ABS, things go a little less dramatically. The plastic pipe cuts well with a hacksaw, and after you have cleaned off the burr with a knife or sandpaper and tried the fit dry (without solvent glue), simply wipe the viscous ABS cement around the male and female ends to be joined, insert and hold for 10 seconds. Do the preplanning slowly and the gluing operation quickly, because the joint sets almost instantly and the bond is unbelievably strong—you can't undo it afterward to put it where you really meant to. (This

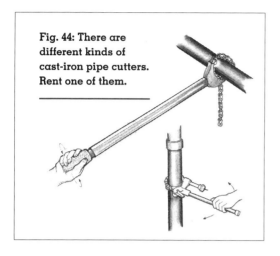

Fig. 44: There are different kinds of cast-iron pipe cutters. Rent one of them.

bears repeating: *You cannot undo an ABS joint. If you make a mistake, you have to cut out the entire connection and throw it away.)*

After all the waste pipes and vents are installed and left jutting out of the wall about 2 inches, cap them off. In many jurisdictions, you'll need to pressure-test for leaks before the inspector will sign off.

▪ S U P P L Y I N G T H E   L I N E S ▪

NOW IT'S TIME TO RUN THE SUPPLY lines. Hot water goes on the left, cold water on the right, except for the toilet supply, which can be on either side of the toilet and is of course cold water. (Everyone has a tale about the plumbing job that was so bad that there was hot water running into the flush tank, and you don't want a story of your own like that.)

Depending on building codes in your area, many of which will allow CPVC inside walls, it may be possible to use rigid plastic

pipe. Connections are made as with ABS, using a special solvent-weld cement. It looks too easy, but there are drawbacks. PVC, meaning polyvinyl chloride, will carry cold water, and CPVC, chlorinated polyvinyl chloride, is rated for hot water, but most codes won't let you put PVC behind or inside walls. Ask your inspector if you can use CPVC for both. If he says yes, he'll also warn you to change the pressure-relief valve on your water heater. Most kick out at 125 psi (pounds per square inch), but CPVC is rated for 100 psi. You see the problem: Your pipe will explode or melt before the pressure-relief safety valve can take the pressure off. Not good.

The cement for CPVC (and PVC, too, for that matter) comes in two cans. The first is a thin, colored liquid, a cleaning agent; the second is clear and sticky, the actual solvent cement. As with ABS cement, it sets quickly and with a vengeance.

Personally, we would use rigid copper, type L, for all supply lines. It cuts easily with a hacksaw or with a lovely little implement called a tube cutter that you can pick up at any plumbing supply center. With practice, you can learn to "sweat" joints. Basically, the process goes like this: After dry-fitting the supply lines—elbows and tees and lengths of rigid copper—together, you shine up all the points of contact so that everything looks like a new penny. (Use emery paper rolled up into a cylinder to get the insides of elbows, tees and couplings.) Smear both ends of the joint with flux or paste or liquid, and then plug them together. Check placement: Make sure the elbow, for example, is facing the correct direction. Now heat the joint with a propane torch, taking great care not to wipe the flame over your wooden studs or ABS waste lines, and then touch the tip of the solder wire to the joint. As soon as the pipe hits the required temperature, the solder will flow into the joint by capillary action, as if sucked into place. Don't overheat the copper; you just want it hot enough to make the solder melt. And of course you'll be using solder that's rated for drinking water; Dad's old solder roll most likely contains unacceptable levels of dangerous metals that will contaminate your clean bathroom water.

By the way, you'll want to cap and test the supply lines as well, using an air pump. If you use water in the lines to test it, you'll have to drain it all out to resolder any bad joints. This might be a good job for your paid plumber, who will be right there if a soldered joint doesn't pass muster. It would be unwise to put drywall over a leaking pipe, be it waste or supply.

Remember to extend or "stub out" all the supply lines 2 inches or so from the finished plane of the walls. That gives you ample clearance to attach the shutoff valves for the lavatory and toilet supply lines. Check that your hot and cold copper pipes do not touch anywhere, and fasten any long runs of pipe to an adjacent joist or stud, using copper brackets available where you bought the pipe. The brackets prevent the pipes from moving and banging, noises you'd recognize from cheap rentals you shared in your youth.

You might also want to insulate the hot water line so that all the heat you pay for in the tank makes it to your sink and tub. There are lengths of foam formed to fit neatly around copper pipe.

Do one final check to make sure that no pipe is situated where a drywall nail or screw can pierce it. If you find such a danger zone, install a steel plate to protect it; you'll bend the drywall nail if you try to drive one there, but better that than to perforate one of your pressurized water pipes.

Fig. 45: Expensive to buy but easy to install, a macerating toilet may be your best bet for a basement water closet.

▪ T O I L E T   T A L K ▪

S--T FLOWS DOWNHILL." SOME SAY that's all you need to know to be a residential plumber. But what do you do at the bottom of the hill? How do you put a toilet in a basement?

In modern subdivision developments, contractors often solve this problem for you by running a house's main sewage line to the sewer from *below* the level of the basement floor (so that the basement is not, in fact, the bottom of the hill). They even rough in basement bathrooms in many cases, installing the drains before pouring the concrete. Unfortunately, for every other house in the world, the sewage line either exits through the basement wall or disappears into the basement floor and then makes a sharp turn toward the sewer or the septic tank. In those cases, if you put a toilet on the floor or a shower or tub, water and waste cannot be made to simply flow away. Don't worry, however; technology once again rushes to your aid.

There are two answers to the problem: One is expensive to buy, the other is expensive to install. Both involve pumps, and neither is terribly satisfying when compared with the elegance of modern plumbing, which in cities at least is entirely gravity-powered and contains no moving parts.

The standard ("expensive to install") solution to the problem of removing waste and water from a basement bathroom is a hefty pump contained in a large, sealed reservoir.

Installation requires cutting through the concrete basement floor and digging a pit deep enough to contain the entire unit, then cutting another hole for the toilet so that waste can exit through a proper trap, and then digging a trench to contain the pipe that carries everything to the tank. The process is messy, requires jackhammers and/or masonry saws, and you'll have to pour concrete when you are done. From then on your basement contains a large drum of sewage and requires a pump—remember Murphy's Law—to empty it on a regular basis into either the sewer system or into your septic tank.

The alternative is something called a "macerating toilet." Macerate, which means to soften, implies something rather more delicate than the actual process going on in these machines, but you get the idea. A small tank, about the size of a narrow picnic cooler, sits on the floor behind the toilet and receives waste from the toilet itself and also from the sink and even a shower or tub (see Fig. 45). All sewage is ground into a liquid or buffeted by jets of water (that's the softening part), then pumped to the main sewage line through a ¾-inch pipe. The small size of that outlet is what makes the system so impressive. Instead of a 3-inch or 4-inch monster taking everything away, sewage is handled by the same-sized pipe that carries water throughout the house. The macerating toilet costs two to three times as much as the in-floor tank and ejector system, but the installation is far simpler and tidier.

POWER TO THE BASEMENT

▪

Wiring the Walls
and the
Ceiling Downstairs

IF YOU NEED TO CONSULT A HOW-TO BOOK IN ORDER to do your wiring, then probably you also need to contact an electrician. Some wiring jobs can be relatively straightforward, such as replacing an outlet receptacle or changing a light fixture. If you are planning extensive alterations to the wiring layout of the basement of your house, however, you will need the advice of an expert. What's more, in many areas you will be required to name your electrician on the application for the permit to do renovations, and you may well be required to have a separate permit for the electrical work itself. This is a no-fooling-around area of concern. Authorities take electrical work extremely seriously, and for good reason. While a mistake in framing may require expensive refitting, and a mistake in plumbing may cause a major domestic flood, mistakes with the electrical circuits cause overheated wires or even sparks and can lead to fires. The consequences are potentially fatal.

People will tell you that if you wire your own house and the unlicensed work causes a fire, the insurance will not cover the dam-

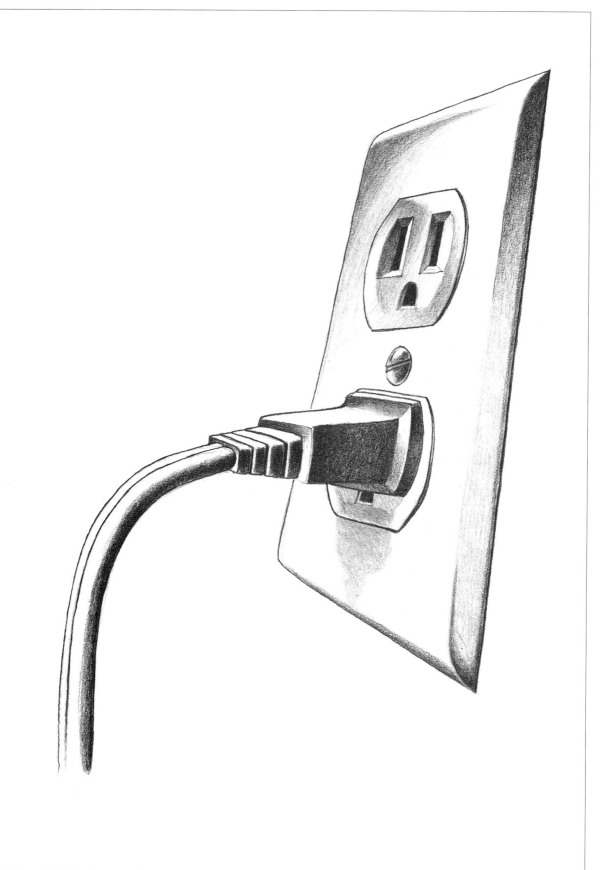

age. But that's not always the case. You may wire your own residence as long as you are living in the space and are not renting it out; however, local authorities might require it to be inspected by a licensed electrician and then inspected again by the local utility. In order to obtain your building permit, you may also be required to sign a document that swears you are going to do the work yourself and not hire a handy, unlicensed friend. If you burn the house down, the insurance will still cover your losses, but they will not repay the money you spent on the wiring job, which seems fair enough.

Even if you don't know what you are doing and plan to hire a professional, there are some things that you should know about wiring. There are also ways you can reduce the cost of the entire project.

First of all, there are codes that govern electrical work. In the U.S., there is the *National Electrical Code*; in Canada, there is the *Canadian Standards Association Electrical Code*. In addition, your municipality, county, state or province may have its own specifications reflecting local conditions. It's important to be aware of which rules apply in your area, and—as with many other such questions—the local building inspection office is the best place to find answers. The electrical permit you need and the two inspections that accompany it—one after the wiring is roughed in (before the drywall goes on) and the other upon completion—will be based on the code requirements that apply to you. A licensed contractor will also be intimately familiar with the rules that apply in the area

where he/she practices. With a little prodding, you will probably be able to start your electrician off on a good long mutter about how fussy the rules are. But they're fussy for a very good reason.

▪SAVING TIME AND MONEY▪

EVEN ASSUMING THAT YOU KNOW little about electricity and are planning to hire a licensed electrician, there are numerous tasks you can do yourself to minimize the costs. Most of these involve pulling wire through holes in the studs and joists or mounting the various boxes necessary for receptacles and switches, overhead lights and junctions. Call around until you find an electrician willing to supervise your efforts, then schedule one short session to go over the job with him or her in order to draw up a list of materials and things to do. Arrange for the electrician to return after you have completed the agreed-upon preparations.

You may also want to purchase the materials yourself if you think you can save money that way, but be absolutely sure you know everything the electrician will want or you'll risk creating an expensive delay during the work. Assume nothing. You need to know, for example, that different kinds of wire are used for baseboard heaters than for wiring receptacles, that there are separate circuit breakers for the heaters and special armored cable for the water heater hookup. There are a million details, and every single one of them is vital if you want your electrician to work without interruption or delay and if you want the inspector to sign off on the work. Once you find an electrician who supports your efforts to save money, you should be entirely up-front. As far as materials go, you'll likely find that your electrician adds a percentage to the cost of any supplies he or she buys at wholesale prices, but in many cases, if the markup is reasonable, the total charge to you will still be less than you will pay at retail prices. If your electrician is being aboveboard, he or she won't mind telling you the amount of the markup.

When you are searching for an electrician, follow the same rules you would for hiring any tradesperson. Ask around; check a few references. Tom has a friend who buys and renovates houses. If you know someone like that, ask who he or she uses and if you can mention his or her name when you call (that way, a little bit of your friend's favored-customer status may rub off on you).

If the house you live in seems to have been well-wired, and if everything is tidy and appears carefully done, check the panel box for a sticker bearing the electrician's name and phone number. It is common practice for electricians to sign their work in this way, and in some areas it is required by law. (This of course works both ways. The man who upgraded the panel in Tom's 135-year-old stone house only a couple of years before he bought it didn't bother bringing the new service in through the stone wall; he chose instead to hack a hole in the beautiful wooden frame of a basement window. It was a careless way to

cut corners. His name is right there on the box, reminding Tom never to call him.)

If you have an older house, one that has undergone a few renovations and upgrades over the decades, you may find that the first wiring problem requiring your attention is the work the last guy did. Wires running at right angles to the ceiling joists and merely stapled on from below will have to be re-strung so that they pass through the joists and are entirely up out of the way. Even if you plan to install furring strips beneath the joists to support tiles or a drywall ceiling, and even if you think that doing so creates enough of a gap for the wire to remain where it is, the danger of someone driving a nail or drywall screw up through that wire will remain until you properly relocate the wire.

To prevent accidental punctures, wires crossing joists should be run through ½-inch to ¾-inch holes that are at least 1¼ inches up from the bottom edge of the joist. The same applies to studs. (Remember that, ideally, all holes go through the center axis of any joists or studs.) That means drilling a lot of holes. It's perfect work for the homeowner to do before the electrician arrives and begins working at $30 per hour. If it is impossible to set the wire back that far, you must drill the hole as far back as possible and install a small metal plate to protect the wire where it passes through the joist. Where wires run parallel to the joists, they can be attached to the side of the joists using either staples or cable straps (see Fig. 46). Wires should be supported every 4 feet or less.

If the wires hanging below the joists dis-

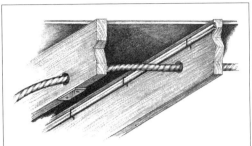

Fig. 46: Wires running parallel to the joists can be attached using staples or cable straps. If an electrical cable runs too close to the edge of a joist or stud, protect the cable with a steel plate.

appear into the ceiling at some point—and almost all of them will, because most wires run up to the floors above—they will have to be disconnected from the main house panel (the fuse box or breaker panel) before you can pull them through their new holes. Again, if you have taken care of these preliminary steps, on the day the electrician arrives everything can be disconnected, rerouted and reconnected at the same time.

The second major time-saver for the electrician is mounting boxes. The wiring is never done before walls are framed in, so by the time you reach this stage of your renovation, the general layout of rooms will be clear to see: Final decisions about the location of lights, receptacles and switches will be easy. Confirm the exact location of each item with your electrician so you don't create any awkward problems and so you meet code requirements. (Receptacles, for example, must be 12 inches from the floor and there must be one every 12 feet.) And when the decisions are made, you can mount all the boxes to wall studs or ceiling joists, as the case may be.

Receptacle boxes and switch boxes can be attached using 3½-inch nails driven through the holes that are provided. Overhead boxes can either be arranged on "hanger bars" that connect between two joists (see Fig. 47) or attached with drywall screws or 1½-inch roofing nails to a short length of 2x4 that bridges the gap between joists. In all cases, the crucial thing to remember is that the edge of the box must be flush with the *finished* surface of the wall or ceiling. That means the boxes must extend past the edge of the stud or joist by the thickness of the drywall or paneling or tiles you plan to use (see Fig. 48).

A trick to remember for later is to always mount your switch and receptacle boxes on the same side of the stud. If you are right-handed, mount them on the right side, because that will be the easiest side to get at when you are hammering. If you do this, then years later, when you want to attach something to the wall, you will be able to locate studs by knowing that they are just to the left of the visible electrical fittings and located at 16 inches on-center from there. (You can turn this trick around as well. Since most people are right-handed, even if you didn't build the room yourself and plan it that way, you can usually find concealed studs just to the left of the receptacles and switches.)

Once the boxes are mounted, you can drill more holes so that everything is ready for the new wire. To take it one step further, go over the layout with your electrician and make a diagram of exactly where all the wires will go, then pull them through yourself so they are ready for the final hookup. Don't be embarrassed about asking lots of questions: You can even have the electrician guide you while you attach strings to remind you where each wire has to go. Some local authorities will require a precise wiring diagram (see Fig. 49) before they'll issue a permit, so you'll have to go over this information with the electrician in any case. You will also have that map to guide you.

After the holes are drilled, pull the wire through the studs and joists, and even into the boxes. Just remember to leave lots of slack at the house panel (4 feet or more—ask the electrician), and wherever wires run in or out of a receptacle or junction box, leave 8 to 12 full inches of wire sticking out so that there is plenty to work with when it is time to connect it all up.

The other thing to remember is that if you are using plastic-coated wire, you must pull it through the holes firmly but gently, and not too fast. Otherwise, when pulling wire through a series of holes, it's possible to get it moving so rapidly that friction melts the sheathing and exposes the copper. This is especially true when you are pulling a second wire through a series of holes that already contain one wire.

When all else is done you can tighten up the cable clamp screw at each box, and even connect the ground wire to the screw provided on each box.

Everything said so far assumes that your local code requires only nonmetallic (NM) sheathed cable (also called #14-2 or #12-2, a reference to the gauge of the wire inside and the fact that there are two wires, a black hot and a white neutral, in addition to the green or bare copper ground). The same suggestions would also apply in areas where the code allows you to use armored cable, the stuff

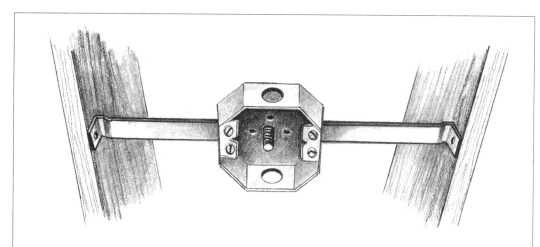

Fig. 47: Special junction boxes with arms are available for installing between joists, or you can purchase hanger bars to support boxes.

with the flexible spiral of metal tubing to protect it (see Fig. 46).

In other areas, however, local standards require that electrical wires be protected by lengths of metal tubing called thin-walled conduit. The conduit is installed and hooked up to all boxes, then wire is pulled through the conduit. It is a job for two people, and requires some experience and a couple of special tools (a reamer and a bender), so you probably won't be able to do it on your own. Instead of hiring someone else, an agreeable electrician should be able to use your labor with this task as well as with helping to "fish" the wires through the installed conduit. You can also do a lot of the busywork—cutting notches in studs and joists and nailing steel plates over those same notches to protect the conduit after installation.

If your basement renovation significantly increases the living area of your house, and es-

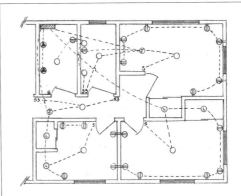

Fig. 49: Your electrical utility may demand a wiring diagram before they'll grant a permit, but you'll want one for future reference regardless.

pecially if you plan to build a new kitchen there or if you plan to install baseboard heating, your present electrical service may not be adequate. Once again, this is something you should discuss with an electrician, but for starters you can have a look at your fuse box or breaker panel and tell right away whether or not there is room for additional circuits. The panels come in a variety of sizes, and the spaces for circuits are punch-out openings on the front plate. If there are unused locations, you will see them immediately (see Fig. 50).

▪ A WORD ABOUT THE GFCI ▪

THERE IS AN ENTIRE MOVIE GENRE OF murder-by-electrical-appliance-in-the-bathwater, and another whole genre of toaster-in-the-tub humor. Everyone knows

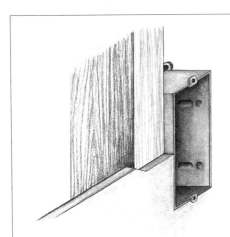

Fig. 48: Outlet boxes should be installed so they will be flush with the finish wall.

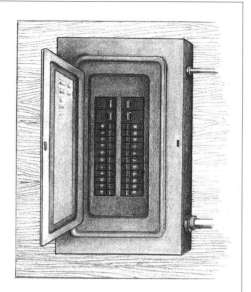

Fig. 50: A circuit breaker box is safer and more modern than a fuse box, and an existing breaker box will often have room for additional circuits.

ceptacle except that it usually has a small red button on the face or a red button and a black button. This receptacle works by detecting even the tiniest changes in the current flowing in and out of a hair dryer or curling iron or shaver. Regular household appliances work by drawing power from one side of the wall receptacle through one of the prongs on the plug you insert, and then returning it through the other prong to the other side of the receptacle. As long as everything is working properly, the same amount of current flows out as flowed in. If, however, you decide to make cheese melts underwater, the extra current that begins to draw off in order to electrocute you will trip a little breaker in the GFCI and shut off the power just like the breakers on the main panel shut down an overloaded circuit. A GFCI works in as little as $\frac{1}{30}$ of a second and can detect differences as small as .006 amperes—not much, in other words.

The GFCIs may be required everywhere in your basement, or just in the areas adjacent to sinks, washers, tubs and showers. This, too, is a matter to discuss with your electrician. Also ask how GFCIs can be wired into a series of receptacles so that one (costly) GFCI will protect the other comparatively inexpensive receptacles downstream (meaning farther along the circuit) from it.

that the deadliest place to be playing with anything electrical is the bathroom, and since it is the presence of moisture that causes that danger, the basement is the second most worrisome place to be handling electrical cords. The safeguard against electrocution in all such cases is something called a ground-fault circuit interrupter (GFCI). In many jurisdictions these are being required in all basement applications.

The GFCI looks like a regular wall re-

YOU LIFT 16 TONS AND WHAT DO YOU GET?

•

*Putting Up the Drywall
and Laying On the Mud*

AFTER THE SOFFITS HAVE BEEN FRAMED, THE plumbing pipes and heating ductwork hidden up between the joists or in chases, the rough wiring finished and after you, the person doing all this work, have had time to rest a little, take another day to plan the drywall. That's right, spend an entire day just getting the procedural strategy worked out in your head—where you'll start, how long you think it will take and any hitches you might encounter—and use this planning time to get physically, emotionally and spiritually prepared.

The first task is to estimate the amount of drywall you'll need to buy. First calculate the total ceiling area in square feet, and then add 20% for soffits and wastage. You won't be able to use up every scrap of drywall sheeting, so assume right now that you'll have to chuck some of it.

Once you've got your square-foot figure, including the extra one-fifth, divide that number by 32, the number of square feet in a

4x8 sheet of drywall. If you get a fractional remainder, round it off on the plus side to the nearest whole sheet. For the ceiling, you'll use ⅝-inch drywall, so write that down as a separate number of ceiling sheets to order.

Now find the square footage of wall surface, including closets, interior partitions and any exterior walls that you have prepared with furring strips. Plan to use ½-inch board this time, and keep a separate list. Again, add 20% and divide the resulting number by 32. The thing to keep in mind is that each sheet will cover a *maximum* of 32 feet—that is, if all the studs or joists are spaced correctly and everything goes perfectly right. Even then, however, full sheets must often be cut into smaller pieces to fit around doors and windows, with a few square feet left over that you won't be able to put anywhere. Toward the end of the job, you can economize and measure every scrap, searching out the ones that are just a little bigger than the remaining gaps in your board. In fact, you *should* do this: Too much waste is as impractical as not ordering enough material. (Professional drywallers often dispose of scraps by placing them inside partition walls. There's nothing wrong with putting that extra material into what is otherwise a hollow wall; it saves on the effort and expense of disposal, both of which can be considerable in these times of overflowing landfill sites and ever-increasing tipping fees. Many municipalities will not take away construction waste at the curb. There is also a growing trend of recycling drywall back to the manufacturer of the product. Check to see if this is an option with your supplier.)

Note that you can buy drywall sheets up to 12 feet in length, but you shouldn't bother with these unless you have lots of wide open spaces to cover. And even if you do, check first to make sure your stairwell is large enough for you to muscle those huge, heavy monsters into your basement. (Tom's isn't.) If you decide to use them, figure out exactly where each such sheet will be used, then order the remainder of the material you'll need in the more manageable 8-foot lengths.

▪ C E I L I N G S ▪

THERE ARE TWO WAYS TO PUT DRY-wall on a basement ceiling: the hard way, and the impossible way. The easy way does not exist, because hanging drywall on a ceiling is strenuous, time-consuming and unpleasant, even when everything goes perfectly. Now that you're apprehensive, let's see how we can best make "lidding" (as professional drywallers call the ceiling phase of drywall installation) your basement ceiling a bit easier.

First of all, do you *have* to use drywall? No. You can, instead, install a dropped ceiling, which is basically rectangles of acoustic tile suspended on a metal framework. These replace the difficulties of drywall with the beauty (and expense) of a tile ceiling. "Oh, damn the cost," you might say. That's the intelligent option: No cutting holes in sheets of drywall for light fixtures or furring around soffits. A dropped ceiling will hide all the mechanical gizmos and keep everything accessible. If a pipe leaks, you just replace a few tiles after the plumber is gone, instead of ripping out soggy drywall and patching it all (seamlessly, expertly) afterward.

However, aside from the expense, which is considerable, not every basement can accommodate a dropped acoustic ceiling for the simple reason that not every basement has enough height to spare. Also, soffits look very

Fig. 51: The easy way to lift and place ceiling drywall is with a hoist. The hard way is with your back.

nice when drywalled, but not so good when covered with a patch job of tiles (although a hybrid *is* possible—drywalled soffits for big protrusions and ceiling tile everywhere else).

Acoustic tile ceiling systems are also not a good do-it-yourself project. Installing them should be left to the experts, people who have put in dozens, if not hundreds, of them. The task *can* be done by amateurs, but will you, for instance, know what to do if your ceiling dimensions do not work out to an even number of tiles? Can you install the metal framework so that it is perfectly level?

Experts will do a good job and back it up with all sorts of guarantees and references, unless they're real fly-by-nights, in which case you should keep looking for a licensed and bonded and *experienced* contractor. After you've laid out a lot of money for a good acoustic ceiling, you don't want beginner baboons practicing on your basement.

Which brings us back to drywall. If you have done a reasonably good job of tucking the pipes, wires and ducts between the joists, you should be able to drywall the whole shebang yourself. If you must call in experts to texture it, or even tape and finish the joints, at least you know that your work—basic drywall hanging—represents a considerable savings of folding money.

When you are about ready to begin, hie down to the rental place and pick up a specially designed machine that lifts drywall sheets into position, with a bed that tilts and can be cranked all the way up to the ceiling (see Fig. 51). You'll be glad you did. Otherwise, you're going to have incredible back, neck and shoulder aches from standing on tiptoe while bending over backward in the yoga position known as "The Drywaller." You'll still have to assume this position to nail or screw each sheet, but you won't have to hold the sheet overhead with your two hands and top of your skull while nailing or screwing it to the joists with your third and fourth hands.

If you want to save some money, you can make up two long tees—long enough to extend from the floor to the finished drywall ceiling plus one inch—out of 2x4 studs, and have another person standing ready to place these under each sheet of drywall, to hold it while you nail it. But you'll have to raise the sheets to the ceiling manually, and that's still a backbreaking job. Go to the rental place, spend the money and write it off as a necessary chiropractic expense.

Keep in mind that drywall sheets go perpendicular to the joists, not parallel to them. Begin at any corner by measuring: Does the 8-foot (or 12-foot) length break over the center of a joist? That's what you want, in theory. In practice, you'll probably need to cut that first sheet at some measurement like 85¼ inches. Make sure the factory-finished edge is out where the next sheet of drywall goes, and the end you cut is against a wall where it will be covered by the drywall that later goes onto the wall. Then, presuming the carpenters did their jobs correctly and the joists are on good 16-inch (or, more commonly, 24-inch) centers, you'll be able to put up entire sheets without cutting them, except for the last one. Go back to your point of be-

Fig. 52: Stagger joints at least one stud space (24 inches) apart, and preferably twice that.

ginning and start the next run, staggering the end joints at least 24 inches but preferably 48 inches (see Fig. 52). Visualize a brick wall and how the courses of bricks are staggered. In the same way, staggering the end joints 4 feet makes a stronger and more even ceiling, although it makes for more taping and sanding and general hardship. You want a good, professional-looking job, something that only *looks* easy.

By the way, we are assuming you know that drywall is cut to size in the following manner: First, mark your line on the front of the sheet, then score over that line with a utility knife so that the paper is cut through. Next, bend the sheet backwards until it breaks neatly along your line, then cut through the paper that remains intact on the back. You knew that?

Presumably, you have laid in a good supply of drywall nails or screws long enough to hang ⅝-inch drywall. In addition, you also should have a good tool, such as a drywall hammer, a cordless drill with a Phillips-head bit or even a genuine drywall gun, for affix-ing these nails and screws. If you want to save money, use drywall nails. These can be placed in a nailing pattern of two nails close together (every 3 inches or so; check the code for your area) so that the first nail secures the sheet of drywall and the second pulls it up tight. Be sure to dimple the nails so that the heads aren't sticking out below the drywall. Put lots of nails on the end joints but not so close to the end that the gypsum breaks apart inside the paper wrapping of the drywall sheet. Wear safety glasses so you don't fill up your eyes with gypsum. (And when the job is fin-ished, make an appointment with a chiro-practor to take the kinks out of your neck.)

Alternatively, you can use drywall screws. This is definitely the way to go if you care more about your neck and shoulders than you do about money. Drywall screws are bugle-headed, self-countersinking and expensive, and they will hold your drywall in place until Judgment Day.

Drywall contractors often use a special belt-fed power tool that puts each screw into the electric drill. This tool is worth renting if you can find it. Even without the fancy gad-get, though, you won't be sorry if you choose not to use nails, especially if your first few sheets need a little realignment. Just flip the lever on your drill or screw gun and reverse the screws out, reposition the drywall and re-place the screws in the sheet. Try *that* with a drywall nail (or three). Nails are cheaper, yes, but they're also extremely unforgiving. Once put in place, screws remain in place and will hold the sheet of drywall securely overhead.

The ceiling drywall will no doubt be per-forated with many openings for light fixtures. These holes are usually circular, and if you don't own the wonderful tool called a drywall compass (a cutting wheel mounted on a slid-ing bar), go out and buy one right away. You'll need to make these circular holes almost ex-actly the right size, one for each junction box, and a keyhole saw just won't do it. No, that's not entirely true: A keyhole saw will do it bet-ter than the impossible way (using a utility knife, for instance), but the openings will be ragged and out-of-round. Believe it: You'll want a drywall compass, plus a few other tools you don't already own (see Tools, page 111). Rent them if you must, borrow them if you can, but get them. Hanging ceiling dry-wall is hard enough without making it an ex-ercise in tool creativity.

Speaking of holes, there is an easy way to determine the location of the circular junc-tion-box holes in your ceiling, where the light fixtures will go. If there are holes to be cut in the first piece of drywall that you will be fit-ting into a corner of the room, begin by mea-suring from the center of the junction box to the nearest point on one of the *side* walls of the basement. Then measure again from the center of the junction box to the nearest point on one of the *end* walls of the basement (you should have two measurements taken at 90-degree angles to each other). On your piece of drywall, mark two lines that represent these same distances (see Fig. 53), and where the lines intersect, set the point of your drywall compass and mark your circle.

At the beginning of this job, on your first

course of drywall sheets, you may luck out and not have any holes to make. But if you do have to make a hole in the first sheet in the corner, you do it by measuring from the walls. Thereafter, you measure from the adjacent sheet(s) of drywall. Set the compass to make a 4¼-inch hole—no tighter than that unless you've done this before many times, and no bigger than that unless you're fond of patching around the rim. Then measure again to make sure you're not transposing the dimensions (Was it 45¾ inches from the end and 17⅛ inches from the side, or the other way around?), and carefully place the compass.

We're assuming you have the sheets stacked conveniently near the point of installation and that your sense of spatial relationships is good enough to mentally move each sheet into position before you pick it up. Practice visualizing how each sheet will go in the ceiling. This is important to stress, because right becomes left when down becomes up, as is the case when you raise a piece of drywall from where you've been working on it on the floor and set it overhead.

Make your scoring cut with the drywall compass in the face of the sheet first, then push a nail all the way through to mark the

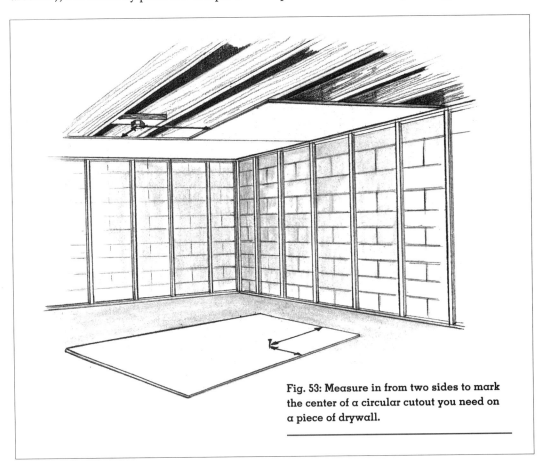

Fig. 53: Measure in from two sides to mark the center of a circular cutout you need on a piece of drywall.

compass point on the back and score the back side. That's how the pros do it. But if you're having trouble transferring the measurements from overhead to underfoot, you can do your measuring and figuring and cutting on the back side of the sheet first. It's not as white as the front of the sheet (prepare to get eyestrain), but it's one way of overcoming the spatial dyslexia all people have some of the time and that some people have all of the time when transferring measurements.

To save time and energy during this difficult phase of drywalling, you need only 10 nails or screws to hold a sheet of drywall to the ceiling initially. Later, you can go back and finish putting your fasteners of choice along the edges and in the "field" (the space between all the edges of the drywall). That way, you aren't dividing your time between hanging and pounding. You can just get those heavy sheets up and out of the way, let your arm and neck muscles recuperate, and do the lion's share of the nailing when you feel stronger. Do not use fewer than 10 fasteners for your temporary nail-up, though: Three should go on each end and four in the field. Once everything is in place, go back and finish off with nails or screws 8 inches apart on every joist.

· W A L L S ·

ONCE ALL THE SHEETS ARE HANGING on the ceiling, it's time to drywall the vertical surfaces: the walls. Put the first course of sheets tight up against the ceiling drywall

(see Fig. 54), then install the bottom course of sheets. Unless 4 feet of clearance remains, you'll have to cut the long side of each lower sheet, the one that almost meets the floor. Allow ⅜ inch of space at the bottom. By orienting the sheets this way, you ensure that the long horizontal joint is as far below most adults' line of sight as is possible. That length of taping can be difficult to do perfectly, but set at that height, imperfections don't show. (At least not as much, anyway.)

Keep the horizontal joints tight by lifting each sheet up from the floor. You can use a flatbar and make-do fulcrum (a 1-foot length of 1x2 will suffice), which is the hard but cheap way, or use a special tool that drywallers like—an aluminum drywall lifter, sometimes called a foot fulcrum (see Fig. 55). It is basically a tiny teeter-totter with a thin steel ledge that slips under the drywall sheet, combined with an integral fulcrum and a knobby surface on which to place your workboot. With either of these, you can raise an entire sheet of drywall tight up against the sheet above with one foot, and nail or screw it off with your two free hands. Flatbar or drywall lifter? Guess which one is easier. It costs around $10 and is worth every penny.

Finally, nail corner bead on all the outside corners of the walls to cover over the rough-cut edges of the drywall and make everything look nice and straight. Corner bead—available wherever you buy drywall—is made of lightweight metal bent to almost 90 degrees. You can nail it in place or use screws, but in either case take great care not to bend or crease the pieces. Also, do not attempt to force the corner bead down flat onto the drywall. The bend in the metal is meant to hold the rounded corner—the "bead"—out a little bit from the planes of the two walls so that the drywall compound that goes on next will cover all the metal.

Most drywall suppliers can also rent you a crimper, a tool that should make the job of setting corner bead idiotproof (but it doesn't always). Once you've set the corner bead in place, you hold the crimper on the bead and strike it with a rubber mallet. The crimper cuts a couple of little points into the corner bead itself and drives those points into the drywall, where they hold like tiny nails.

When you are finished hanging the drywall, take a break. Take several. It's brutal work, but you have covered all the ceiling joists and the furring on the walls, as well as the framing for soffits and support posts. (You didn't drywall over any vents in the sides of the main ducts, did you?) The entire basement will have an odd echo now; revel in it. Let the irrational surges of joy well up into your bosom, and briefly entertain the thought that you're done, that you could stop right now and fly to the Bahamas for a month.

▪ FINISHING ▪

OKAY, IN TRUTH YOU *ARE* ALMOST DONE, and certainly you are over the hard part. Now you're going to make your walls and ceiling seamless. The first step is to tape the joints.

Arguments rage over the proper type of tape to use: paper—the choice of professional

Fig. 54: The first course of drywall goes tight up against the ceiling drywall so that irregularities in the long joint lie well below the view of the average adult.

drywallers—or sticky mesh? We would not dream of endorsing either product, were it not for the fact that at least one of us has had decades of experience with both kinds of joint tape. Here are the pros and cons of each.

Paper tape is cheaper, and it comes in huge rolls. You apply it by laying down a narrow, thin "bed coat" of drywall compound ("mud") on the joint and then unrolling the paper tape into the mud immediately.

Let us pause here to point out an important feature of drywall sheets: Along the long sides of every sheet, the gypsum is thinned so that when two sheets are set side by side, the joint lies in a shallow valley. The drywall compound and the tape are set down into this recess, so they're easy to hide completely (see Fig. 56). The shorter ends of the sheets are called the butts and have no such feature. It's more difficult to create an invisible joint right on the flat surface of the drywall, and for that reason, drywallers (and you) always want to avoid butt joints. This is why it's best to use the longest possible sheets for your job.

Drywall joint compound comes pre-mixed and in large boxes or 5-gallon pails for major jobs such as yours, so don't confuse what you want with powders that you've mixed up for minor patches in the past. You begin by troweling the compound into the recessed joint, then measuring out enough paper tape to do the whole length of a joint. One pass with the trowel embeds the tape into its bed coat and sets it flush with the surface of the drywall.

Where the ends of the sheets are not beveled and you are forced to make a butt

Fig. 55: An aluminum foot fulcrum will help to lift the second (lower) course of drywall off the floor.

joint, you'll have to get good at a process known as "feathering," which is hiding the hump created by the tape (see Fig. 57). In order to feather a joint, you apply progressively thinner and wider coats of joint compound, sanding the edges between each coat. Eventually, the joint is covered by an extremely thin coat of joint compound whose edges disappear into the paper coat of the drywall. When done properly, it's all quite elegant.

If the tape doesn't want to adhere to the bed coat, as sometimes happens, it will bubble. You can fix this by letting everything dry, then cutting out the bubbles with a razor, filling in the small holes with a dab of compound and troweling it smooth. Once the compound dries, you lightly sand the patch until it blends into the bed coat.

But let's suppose that the paper tape does not decide to bubble, that it instead lies flat and does what it's supposed to do. You must wait until the bed coat dries, then use the trowel to break off any ridges or bumps that might put hard little knots into your next

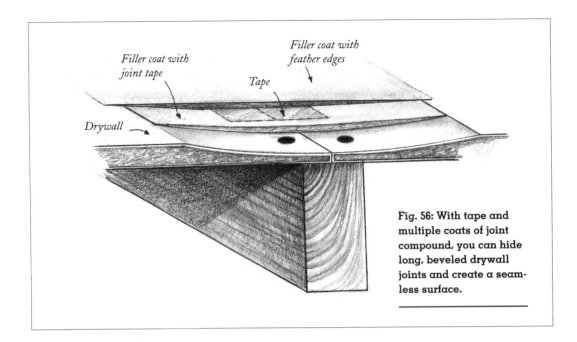

Filler coat with joint tape

Filler coat with feather edges

Tape

Drywall

Fig. 56: With tape and multiple coats of joint compound, you can hide long, beveled drywall joints and create a seamless surface.

coat. Then sand lightly and apply another coat of joint compound. Wait until that coat dries, sand lightly again, and lay on yet another coat, this time using a very wide (10-inch to 12-inch) trowel. You have now applied three coats of "mud" to every joint, and the beveled joints in particular are very smooth and flat. After one more dose of sanding, making certain that every edge is feathered to perfection—use your hand and eye to ensure this—you're ready to apply texture or paint.

That's the story for paper tape. One warning, however: Do not oversand at any of these stages. You don't want to expose the tape and rough it up with sandpaper, or you'll be set back one whole step.

Mesh tape, on the other hand, merely requires you to press it on, sticky side down like masking tape, over every joint—a clean, dry process that involves nothing more than a knife to cut the mesh to the correct lengths. With that done, kick back with a cup of coffee until you feel like mixing the gooey stuff, then start laying down the coats of joint compound. Mesh tape is more expensive than paper tape, but a lot easier to put on. It's fantastic for patching holes, too.

Which would we recommend for the do-it-yourselfer? We won't say, but we've left you several clues.

CORNERS

FOR INSIDE CORNERS, WHERE TWO walls meet or where walls meet the ceiling, you need to fold the mesh tape along its length and press it tightly into the corner with the edge of your trowel. If, for your own reasons, you are using paper tape, lay mud on both surfaces (wall and ceiling, for example), then set the tape—folded along its length—in place and squeegee away the excess mud as you do with any other joint. Let all this set, then do the next coat *on only one of the surfaces*—say, the wall. That way, you'll be able to use the other surface (in this case, the ceiling) as a guide for your knife. When that coat has set up, switch it around and do the second coat on the ceiling, using the wall to guide the side of your knife. Carry on in this way until all your coats are on.

Now turn to the corner beads you fixed to all the outside corners. If you mounted them correctly, you'll notice that the bead stands out a mite from both flanges of the corner bead and therefore from the surfaces that meet at that corner. Just let the metal guide your knife as you fill in that mite and feather it farther and farther from the corner (see Fig. 58).

There are two types of compound for finishing drywall: Joint compound, self-explanatory, is for joints. It has lots of glue in it and no longer contains asbestos, as it did a long time ago. It is a nightmare to sand. Topping compound, by contrast, is easy to sand, and it is used for the final coat (or coats, if it comes to that) that paves over everything and makes it smooth. The process of applying wet compound and sanding it when dry is so arduous that you will be on-your-knees grateful for topping compound's ease of sanding. Putting a feather edge on it is a snap, although by this stage in the proceedings you will be so consumed by your hatred of sanding that you may not notice or care how wonderfully topping compound can be smoothed out. By the way, use either a piece of scrap lumber as a large, flat sanding block or invest in a drywaller's sanding pole, a handy imple-

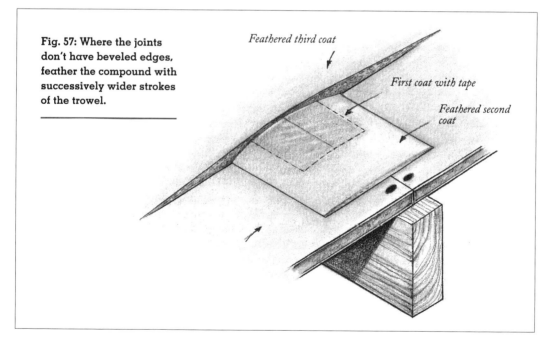

Fig. 57: Where the joints don't have beveled edges, feather the compound with successively wider strokes of the trowel.

Feathered third coat

First coat with tape

Feathered second coat

ment that makes the job much easier. *Always* wear a dust mask, no matter what kind of sanding block you use. This is another of those pieces of advice that bears repeating: Wear a good dust mask, just as the professionals do.

Drywall compound comes as a ready-mixed paste. Some drywallers prefer to homogenize it further to make it more workable: They add compound and a little water into a big white bucket, and stir it with a *bladed* or *cage* paddle and a good-sized drill until it is the consistency of thick pancake batter. Adding a cup of latex bonding agent, a white liquid that is basically more glue, helps joint compound adhere to walls and ceilings and minimizes cracking. For simple joints, however, you probably don't need to add anything.

After all your sanding is done, there will be a fine white dust everywhere you worked (and throughout the rooms above, too, unless you thought to tape plastic over doors and shut off furnace ducts to prevent the spread). Do *not* use your vacuum cleaner to suck up this mess: The fine particles will clog the filter and can also damage the motor. And do not start pushing the dust everywhere with a broom, creating clouds of confusion. Instead, either purchase sweeping compound (the stuff you probably remember the janitor using when you were in school), or if you have sawdust saved up from other work, place it in a garbage bag and mix it with enough water so it is thoroughly dampened; then spread that everywhere and sweep it up. The dust will stick to the sawdust and tidy up nicely.

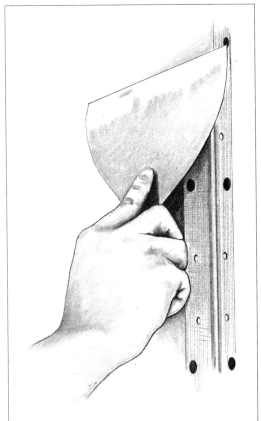

Fig. 58: Hold one side of the trowel against the metal bead and pull the joint compound downward to fill an outside corner.

If you have finished the drywall to an utterly flat surface, you are now ready to paint or hang wallpaper. But perhaps you want to hide minor glitches and make all your surfaces a little more interesting. Texture can be blown on by a machine, available at most rental outlets, or even applied by hand if you know what you're doing. Do not, as some people suggest, add cornmeal to paint, unless you want to create a wall surface like sandpaper. Nor should you smear on joint compound and work it around with a comb; it will look awful. What the experts do is add sand to joint compound and put little globs of it everywhere in random patterns with a sponge, and then flatten out the high spots with a wide trowel in large sweeping motions. We should hasten to point out that, yes, experts do this, but not their apprentices. If you decide you want to try it, however, start in a back room or closet, or experiment on a sheet of scrap drywall. If the result pleases you, go from there.

▪ T O O L S ▪

IN ADDITION TO THE TOOLS WE'VE ALready mentioned, here's what you'll need:

Four trowels (commonly called drywall knives, for some obscure reason, and that's what you may have to ask for at the hardware store) will suffice: a taping knife, 4 to 6 inches wide, for putting the first coat of joint compound under the paper tape (or over the mesh tape); a fairly flexible 8- to 10-inch trowel for the next coat; the extremely flexible 12- to 16-inch-wide trowel, sometimes called a blue-steel knife, for the final coat; and a handy corner taping knife, for you-know-what: taping inside corners.

The joint and topping compound go in a drywall pan, something else you'll need to pick up at the hardware store. These are made of galvanized steel or plastic with a thin steel edge that fits into a groove along one side, very convenient to carry around and designed for scraping the goo off your trowel. A plastering hawk is not really necessary, but if you decide to apply your own ceiling texture instead of blowing it on, it's indispensable. (The "hawk" is just a flat surface with a handle on it.)

You'll also need a drywall saw, a big-toothed handsaw with hardened teeth that looks nothing like a common handsaw. The handle is often made of plastic, and the blade is very stiff. A drywall T-square is a time-saver for cutting sheets of wallboard. It's 4 feet long and about 22 inches wide across the top of the T, and is made of flat aluminum. You can use it to mark off the electrical box cutouts as well, for a perfect job.

Buy a good utility knife with a retractable blade, handy for everything from cutting joint tape to cutting sheets of drywall. In fact, buy two, because when you mislay one, all work stops. You'll also need a pair of tin snips, for cutting metal corner bead. A chalk line will help you locate the joists, studs and strapping, if you decide to temporarily tack up the drywall and then go back later to nail it off more securely. And don't forget a flatbar, which can be used to pry drywall into tight corners and generally adjust each sheet, as well as an emergency fulcrum in case you mislay your magic drywall lifter.

SLABS
TO SLEEPERS,
POLY
TO PARQUET

∎

Worship the Subfloor
You Walk On,
Then Drop to Your Knees
and
Install the Tiles

A DRY, LEVEL AND PROPERLY FINISHED CON-
crete floor in a basement is a wonderful gift to
you from the contractor who built your house.
Proper drainage at the footings, polyethylene
beneath the floor as a barrier to any hydrosta-
tic moisture and to radon, and a level, polished surface provide you
with a starting point that simplifies every task that follows. You
can be duly grateful. If, however, you were not the recipient of such
a boon—if there are problems of any kind with your basement
floor—now is when you get down on your hands and knees and
investigate thoroughly, because now is when you make your final
meticulous repairs.

▪ L A Y I N G
T H E
G R O U N D W O R K ▪

FIRST, YOU MUST DEAL WITH MOISTURE (see Chapter Two). If water is coming up through the floor, you either have to figure out how to redirect it or you have to create a barrier.

It is possible that runoff water in your area is making its way under your floor and is then wicking up through the concrete. If most of the water you see is at the perimeter of the building, or if you only find seepage during spring runoff, better drainage at the footing may cure the problem. On the other hand, if you have water underneath your building because your basement extends below the water table (or for any of a number of other reasons), the best you can do is block the water from rising through the floor by laying down plastic and perhaps even pouring a second concrete floor over the film. There are contractors who specialize in basement water problems, and you will be wise to pay for some advice before proceeding. Be sure to find a reputable company, however, and keep in mind that you can also gather excellent information about soil conditions in your area and the level of the water table with a call to your local building inspector's office.

If your floor is dry, you can consider a variety of options for finishing the floor. For starters, you can paint concrete. Paints for basement floors have improved over the last several years because there are now durable floor paints with an acrylic latex base. For-merly, wear-resistant floor paints had to be oil-based or rubber-based, and since such products form an impermeable skin on the painted surface, even minute amounts of moisture trapped in the concrete could bubble the paint back off the floor. Latex paints, on the other hand, let small amounts of moisture pass back through without suffering (which is why you can also get away with applying latex paint to wood that is not fully dried). Even if your basement has never had any infiltration of water, the concrete may contain some moisture from condensation. An acrylic latex coating is the way to avoid problems.

Don't assume that bare concrete will just soak up the paint, however. Concrete requires its own special preparation, and you must begin by cleaning up *all* dust and dirt. Since a stain on the floor caused by any kind of oil absolutely will not accept latex paint, you may have to go so far as to chip away a layer of the concrete and refinish the spot, or use acetone or TSP (trisodium phosphate) to eat out the oil stain. And no matter what the floor surface looks like, rough or smooth, it will have to be etched with muriatic acid or a similar proprietary product so that the paint will adhere properly. If your floor is a highly polished concrete, you also will have to scuff the surface with sandpaper. Those are the basics. You may also have to thin the first coat of paint, which for latex paints means adding some water.

Keep in mind, however, that paints—or coatings, as some industry people now generically refer to all the stains and paints and alternatives—are being changed constantly. You need to understand the particular instructions for whatever product you buy. Don't assume anything. When Tom was a kid, he did a paint job for a man who had purchased expensive one-coat gelled paint. It was designed to be the consistency of pudding, but since it didn't look like regular paint, the first thing his boss did—over Tom's squeaky protestations—was to pour in enough paint thinner to cut it down to his idea of a quality finish. As Tom was laying on the third coat and wondering about a fourth, the boss allowed as how he probably should have left it alone. (Should have read the instructions, was what Tom thought, taking a certain unworthy satisfaction in his boss's mistake. This, after all, was the same man who had mortified his budding handyperson's sensibilities when Tom was working on or near the docks by tying tools to his wrist so that they couldn't fall into the water.)

The best way to ensure that you are getting a good product and appropriate instructions is to ask careful questions at a couple of specialty paint stores and to then listen to what the clerks have to say before making a decision. Read the instructions religiously. If they don't seem to jibe with what store personnel are telling you, clear up the confusion before you start. If you aren't satisfied with the answers you are getting, go elsewhere.

Back in Chapter Two, we discussed the practice of laying plastic down on the concrete before installing the floor. Polyethylene plastic serves two purposes in a basement: It prevents moisture in the concrete from soaking into other building products above, and it prevents radon gas present in the soil beneath your house from making its way through the basement floor and into your living space. It is an effective technique in either application.

Before you decide to lay plastic, however, you have to make a decision about flooding in your basement. Tom grew up in a house that flooded to a depth of more than a foot at least twice during his childhood. These were very exciting incidents for him, for he got to wear his rubber boots indoors, and he remembers them (both the incident and the boots) with great fondness. They were also exciting times for his parents, who remember the scenarios somewhat differently. If your house, or your neighbors,' has ever flooded, you want to be very careful about the flooring option you choose for a basement. Unless you can identify the reason for the flood and guarantee it will never happen again, you don't want to build up the floor with wood and plywood and carpet, and you don't want to interfere in any way with installed floor drains.

If your basement *might* flood in the future, fill all cracks with concrete or caulking, then paint the floor and use area rugs. That way, if you have a flood, you'll only have to worry about ruined walls and furniture. A built-up floor that suffers a flood will heave and buckle and twist, then become a garden for all manner of minute fungi and mold.

If you're confident you've dealt with any moisture problems for the last time, now—with the ceiling and all the walls painted and textured but before the toilet is installed in your downstairs bathroom—you can go ahead and install the floor covering.

▪ CERAMIC TILE ▪

OF ALL THE FLOOR COVERINGS AVAILable for the basement, none surpasses ceramic tile for durability. These are not the thin, shiny tiles that go on bathroom walls, but textured tile or pavers that will withstand heavy traffic for years. Carpet is softer, wood parquet is warmer, vinyl tile is somewhat cheaper, but the first two require a framework of wooden sleepers and a strong subfloor, and the last needs a satin-smooth finish on the concrete floor.

If you have the average poured concrete basement floor, its surface will lie somewhere along the spectrum from shiny smooth to screeded off and rough-troweled. For those whose floors are rougher, ceramic tile may be the best option.

Tile imparts an expensive look, but it may be less expensive than good carpet or wood parquet when the savings of your labor is factored in and the cost of materials for a subfloor are discounted. Tile is easy to clean and is virtually permanent. And if your basement includes a solarium of any kind or faces south, a tile floor will absorb the rays of sunlight like a heat sink, subtly warming your basement at night. Perhaps most important, ceramic tiles can withstand any number of soakings and remain good as new. Even if you know your basement will never flood through the walls or floor, there remains the possibility that a burst pipe or similar mishap in the floors above could transform your basement into a giant catch basin. Simply because of its location, the odds are always greater that you'll see water damage downstairs, and if the floor is broadloom over plywood and wooden sleepers, water can soak right in and cause a permanent and ever-smellier mess. (But no matter *what* floor you lay down, if ever there is a flood in the basement, bail and mop, then rent the biggest, meanest skin-desiccating, factory-strength dehumidifiers you can get your hands on and dry everything out to the aridity of a desert.)

A concrete slab makes an excellent base for ceramic tile. The traditional method of setting tiles in a thick bed of mortar at one time limited tile installation to skilled professionals, but a new generation of thinset mastics has changed all that. You still need to clean and prepare your floor surface and preplan your tile placement, but by working carefully and following manufacturer's directions, you can lay a ceramic tile floor that will be indistinguishable from one laid by an expert. We know because we've done it ourselves, though neither of us has ever earned a paycheck laying down foot-square terra cottas.

To begin, the working surface must be clean, relatively smooth and utterly dry. If your basement floor fits this description now or can be made to do so, fine. If you have an uneven or badly cracked concrete basement floor, consider applying tile to a plywood subfloor on sleepers. Sheets of ¾-inch exterior-grade plywood can make an adequate base for ceramic tile, provided that there is no "give" (flexion) anywhere. You should use glue and ring- or screw-shanked nails to affix the subfloor to the sleepers. If the floor already has a layer of—heaven forbid—carpet glued to the concrete, you might be tempted to just build a new wooden platform right over it. *Don't.* You are better off using that same energy to scrape up the offending covering, complete with all the muck that's sifted into it over the years, and throwing it away. If the subfloor is in good shape, lay ceramic tile on that. If the subfloor you uncover is *not* smooth and unbroken, you can put down sleepers and plywood. Whatever you find, you won't have wasted your time: It's always best to start fresh and not heap new floors on top of old. Besides, every floor thickness you add reduces your available headroom.

Whether you start with new plywood or clean concrete, there are, for our purposes at least, two kinds of thinset adhesives: mastics and cement-based. (Epoxy is a third kind, but it's expensive and is best applied by professionals.) Your choice depends on the kind of tile you want to lay, the condition and/or type of subfloor and the recommendations of the tile manufacturer. This is a good time to solicit the opinions of your tile supplier, who can suggest the best product and technique for your situation. If you are working with a wooden subfloor, for example, you may be advised—depending on the type of adhesive you choose—to add another ⅛ or ¼ inch of plywood and to leave narrow gaps between sheets to allow the wood to expand when it soaks up moisture from the glue.

Unless you're extremely lucky, you'll probably have to cut some tiles. A tool rental place can furnish a heavy-duty tile cutter for about $20 a day. You'll need eye and hearing protection to run a motorized cutter, and a little practice beforehand can save you a lot of grief later. If you have any doubts at this point, you may be better off having a professional do the work.

You will want to know exactly how many full and partial tiles are going to be needed. This is the time to do the calculations, so you don't have one-fourth of a tile at the edge of one wall and three-fourths of a tile at the other. Measure out from two opposite basement walls to find the exact center of the basement, and snap a chalk line. Now find the same midpoint from the perpendicular walls and snap another chalk line through that. This cross will intersect in the middle of your floor. This is where you'll begin.

Lay one course of tiles down—don't use cement yet—leaving sufficient space for grout, until you come to both ends. The remaining space, if any, will be the width of your cut tiles. Before you actually cut any tiles, though, make adjustments, in the width of your grout, for example, and work out any patterns in the tile. Include the grout line—the space adjacent to the tiles—in your figuring right from the start. Decide the width in advance and find precise spacers (pieces of wood, usually) to use as you lay successive rows, but be flexible if needed. For instance, if you find you are going to have to trim ½ inch from every edge tile, a better solution may be to go with a narrower joint. By squeezing the

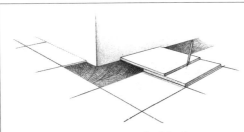

Fig. 59: An accurate method for fitting the last course of tiles along a wall.

grout lines just $1/16$ inch tighter, you'll make up an entire inch with every 16 rows.

As you lay out the tiles, keep in mind that your basement floor may not be perfectly square. *Do not* cut all your edge tiles at once on the assumption that this dimension is the same everywhere. You can check the room for square by measuring the diagonals: The distances between the two sets of opposite corners should be exactly the same. But even if the room *is* square, the walls may bow slightly, so do your tile cutting as you go.

Cutting edge tiles to fit is actually simpler than it might seem. Once the next-to-last row of tiles is in place, follow these steps (see Fig. 59):

1. Place the tile you want to cut (we'll call it T1) directly on top of the row you just installed.

2. Slide the tile (T1) so that it overhangs the previous row by exactly the width of the grout joint.

3. Place another tile (T2) of the exact same size on top of the tile that you want to cut (T1), positioned so that its far edge is touching the wall or is as close to the wall as you want it to be.

4. Trace a line where the T1 crosses T2, and cut along that line. The chunk that you cut off will exactly fill the space between the last row and the wall.

Now you're ready to set the tiles. Begin from the center and spread enough adhesive to do three or four tiles. Follow the instructions and your tile supplier's recommendations for the thickness of the adhesive; usually, you'll be spreading it with a notched trowel (see Fig. 60). The adhesive should be applied so that only a minimal amount will squeeze out into the grout zone when you push the tile down with a twisting motion, but it should be thick enough so that the entire back of the tile is covered. If you have a good eye, you can keep your grout lines straight in two directions; if not, snap guide lines on the floor and follow them, or use light boards to align the edges of your tile. *Do not* walk on the tiles after you've set them, for it may throw the tiles off the grout lines you want to follow, and once the adhesive has started to set, any movement can destroy the bond. A tile layer we know has a story about an assistant who, at quitting time, thought he'd sneak across the finished room instead of going around to get his coat. In the morning there was a trail—left foot, right foot, left foot—of loose tiles that he'd stepped on. Allow tiles to set and cure undisturbed.

The final step of laying ceramic tile is grouting. Again, consult with your tile supplier for the best grout for your application. What you will be buying is some dry form of cement premixed and packaged with various types of adhesives and other polymers that have been added to increase stickiness and flexibility. You mix grout yourself by adding water and stirring it all together in a 5-gallon pail. Use a rubber trowel to apply it, moving the trowel in a diagonal wiping motion across the face of the tiles, forcing the grout into the joints until it entirely fills the spaces between tiles. After you've passed over with the trowel, leaving the surface of the tiles as clean as you can, squeegee off the excess. A clean, damp rag and water that you change regularly works well for this. Once the grout has set and dried, you'll notice a dusty sheen on all the tiles: Clean the surface of the tiles again by buffing with a clean, damp cloth.

Two warnings: First, read the instructions on the bag of dry grouting material and pay close attention to recommendations about how much grout to mix at a time, and about the desired consistency. You may have seen someone else grouting a floor, either in person or on TV, and observed that the mix was so stiff it looked almost dry. If that's not what the instructions call for, you can wear yourself out trying to work with the material improperly mixed. This advice is based on recent painful experience.

Second, buy a new, good-quality grouting trowel. The soft rubber base can stiffen with age and become unable either to work the grout into the gaps or to squeegee the tiles clean. You want a trowel with *both* a layer of spongy material and a bottom layer of stiffer neoprene.

After the grout cures (once again, consult the instructions for times), seal everything with a silicone-based sealer.

▪ R E S I L I E N T ▪
V I N Y L   T I L E S ▪

RESILIENT TILE CAN BE LAID OVER smooth concrete or a wooden subfloor, although the latter requires an underlayment of tempered particleboard. It can even be laid over old tile, as long as the first layer is firmly attached to the basement floor, with

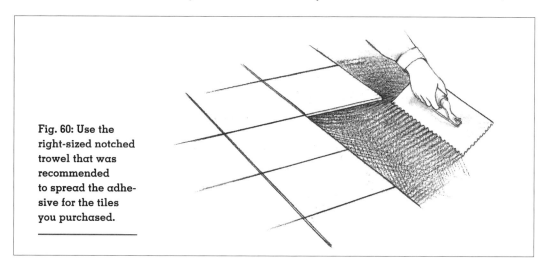

Fig. 60: Use the right-sized notched trowel that was recommended to spread the adhesive for the tiles you purchased.

no loose tiles. Resilient tile is less expensive than ceramic tile, but it's comparatively less durable as well. It is also much easier to install, comes in a wider variety of colors and designs, and may be textured or even cushioned. Many products are self-stick, with adhesive already on the back and a protective paper coat to cover it: These types are extremely simple to lay.

The floor must first be smoothed with spackle, a paste specifically made for filling in holes and cracks. In addition, if there are oil stains or paint, concrete floors must first be cleaned with detergent. Painted floors should be scratched with sandpaper to ensure adhesion.

If you are going to cover an old layer of tile, check to see if any of the tiles are loose. If many are, it may be worth your time to chip them up. Under no circumstances, however, should you remove a previous layer of tiles with a sander, as old tiles can contain asbestos. In fact, unless you are absolutely sure that the tiles are safe, consult an asbestos professional about any removal that you plan.

Once everything is ready, you'll need to find the exact center of the floor and with a chalk line make a cross through it. Put a row of tiles along one axis, *without adhesive*. Just as with ceramic tile, you're trying to find out what size of partial tiles you'll need at the edges. Your task is made a little easier here because you won't have to worry about grout lines: You can butt each tile up against its fellow or sister until the total space is covered.

Adhesive usually comes in cans, and should be applied when the room is warm; cold adhesive will not bond, and it will have the consistency of frozen lard. Read the directions on the side of the can, which will likely suggest that you use a notched trowel with ⅛-inch grooves. Adhesive should not ooze up between the tiles, but no matter how careful you are, some will anyway. Usually any excess can be removed at the end of the job, and the directions on the can will specify a cleanup solvent. The drying time of adhesives will vary, though, so you may wish to clean up the tiles as you go.

Start at the corner farthest from the door, and work slowly. If you lay down guide lines with a chalk line before you begin, your layout will be easy to track, and each course of tiles will stay straight. (Vacuum up any excess chalk *before* you start applying the adhesive. You just want enough to see clearly.) Spread enough adhesive for four tiles at a time (unless you are using self-stick tiles). Some mastics require a set-up time before you can place tiles. Following the supplier's and manufacturer's directions will save you a lot of grief. Don't become discouraged when you realize that the mastic you spread inevitably hides exactly the line you want to set the tile on. Rather, plan to place the tiles and to then check their location by measuring to the next line over.

Make cuts around doors and pipes with a vinyl knife (carefully warming the tile first with a heat gun), or use a jigsaw with a fine blade. Cut the tile and place it dry, making adjustments as needed *before* you apply adhesive, not after. You want a good fit, but not a force fit.

When all the tile is laid and the excess adhesive is wiped off, you may need to rent a heavy roller and go over it. This presses all the vinyl tile down onto the mastic and leaves a smooth surface; the corners of some types of vinyl tile have a tendency to "float" at the joints otherwise. If mastic gets on the roller, clean it off immediately, or you will be charged exorbitantly by the rental place. And a final word of caution: The roller may look quite portable, but it weighs enough to damage your back if you lift it without help.

▪ C A R P E T I N G ▪

BY FAR THE MOST COMFORTABLE floor covering, carpet is easy to lay on a wood subfloor with the proper tools (and experience). It can also be laid over fairly smooth concrete, but the tack strips that hold its edges must then be affixed somehow without nails. This means construction adhesive and powder-actuated guns or screws with anchors. It's not fun, but it's possible.

If you have wood subfloors, begin by installing tack strips, with the hooks facing the walls. A tack strip looks like an implement of torture—like a yardstick studded with hundreds of short nails set at an angle. They are available wherever you buy floor coverings. Cut carpet padding to fit between the tack strips and staple it down every 2 feet or so, so it won't bunch under the carpet. Finally, roll out the carpet so that the seams will not be in high-traffic areas and stretch it with a carpet stretcher (a weird-looking device with claws on one end and a big pad on the other). Crawl around setting the claws at the perimeter of the material and then kicking that big pad with your knee so that the edges of the carpet hook tightly onto the tack strips. Cut away any excess at the walls, join seams with a special hot-glue tape and a carpet layer's iron and you're done.

It sounds quite easy, doesn't it? In practice, laying carpet can be very difficult. Unless you have laid carpet before or are able to work with someone who has, consider having your basement carpet laid by a professional. A carpet supplier will often include installation in the price, and this is definitely a good point to haggle over. Ask yourself if it's worth the headache of doing it yourself, especially after you've done all the other work.

When your flooring of choice is laid down and any adhesives have set, you are basically finished. Buy some simple baseboard and install it, and—unless you chose carpet—disguise the junction of the baseboard and floor with lengths of quarter-round trim. Then you are done. Everything that's left, including fixtures, towel rods and curtains, is merely decoration. And if you're like most renovators, you'll want to spend at least a few years getting around to that stuff.

Now, before you let anyone in to see it, lie down on the floor and take one long satisfied look around, then go call the kids. Get them started on something loud, and when they're not looking, sneak off up to the quiet kitchen. If you installed a door at the top of the stairs, shut it. Basement renovation is its own reward.

GLOSSARY

Anchor bolt: A threaded bolt, usually with a J-shaped end, that protrudes from the foundation through the treated wooden sill immediately above. These bolts anchor the frame of the house to the foundation.

Armored cable: Flexible metal conduit, usually aluminum, that looks like a spiral metal jacket and contains electrical wires that connect a junction box to an appliance such as a water heater. The cable protects the 220-volt wire from damage. Also called Greenfield, BX or Flex.

Bearing/nonbearing: A wall is either a (load) bearing wall or a nonbearing partition, depending on whether or not it supports the weight of the house above it. Bearing walls go perpendicular to joists overhead, or touch two or more joists; nonbearing partitions are parallel to joists.

Bed coat: Refers to the initial "bed" of joint compound on taped edges of drywall, into which paper tape is laid; also, the first coat of joint compound laid over mesh tape.

Bladed and cage paddles: A bladed paddle is a drill-driven paddle with flat blades to cut through and homogenize the joint compound. A cage paddle is shaped like a circular cage and mixes in a different way, efficiently pulling up solids from where they have settled and suspending them in a solution, and therefore is a better choice for certain kinds of paint.

Butt joint: A simple joint formed by butting one wooden member against another; the weakest type of joint. Also refers to the joint formed where the ends (not the longer sides) of two pieces of drywall meet.

Carriage: In a stair system, the main notched 2x12 that holds the treads and risers.

Casing: Finish trim that goes against walls and door/window jambs, covering the gap between the jambs and the rough opening.

Closet flange: The toilet part mounted on the floor where the toilet bowl bottom opening goes, with inside diameters the size of the soil pipe. Used in conjunction with a wax ring.

Cold chisel: A type of cold-rolled steel chisel specifically made for cutting metal such as bolts and useful for cutting concrete.

Construction adhesive: There are numerous products available for use as construction adhesives. They have different names, depending on the retail outlet. Whatever the product is called, for your basement needs it should come in a tube that fits a standard caulking gun; be some form of wood by-product and polymer glue; and be fast-bonding, waterproof and suitable for use indoors. Also, it should be specifically described as remaining flexible once it sets. Find a product that is "Rated for Construction," and be sure that you do not purchase similar adhesives (often made by the same companies) that are intended for gluing foam board insulation to concrete walls—unless, of course, that is what you are planning to do with it.

Corner bead: The perforated metal angle that covers the outside corners of drywall, protecting them from damage.

Course: A contiguous row, as in bricks, shingles, tile and sheets of drywall.

Crimper: A tool that, when placed over a section of corner bead and struck with a rubber mallet, attaches the corner bead by cutting little teeth from the metal and driving them into the drywall.

Cripples: A type of stud, joist or rafter that is not full length, being "broken" (stopped or headed) by a header or sill.

Dropped ceiling: A suspended ceiling, often acoustic tile, that conceals the true ceiling above it; used to hide mechanical systems or to lower a ceiling to an ordinary nominal height of 8 feet.

Drywall/gypsum board/wallboard: Synonyms for a sheet-type wall covering made by pressing a gypsum core in a sandwich of paper facing. Available in different thicknesses.

Dry well: A hidden hole some distance from your house, filled to the brim with gravel, into which your graywater or eaves runoff goes via pipe.

Efflorescence: In the building trades the word refers to a white crust or powder on the surface of brick or concrete walls, caused by the action of water on mineral salts.

Feathering: The process of creating an invisible feather-thin edge of drywall compound at joints. The feather edge disappears into the field of the drywall sheet.

Flatbar: A flat steel bar, curved at one end; useful for a million jobs including prying boards apart, adjusting door jambs and raising the bottom course of sheets of drywall off the floor and tight against the joint on the upper course.

Floor flange: See CLOSET FLANGE.

Footing: The long concrete pad making contact with the earth at the bottom of a foundation, upon which the entire house rests.

Framing square: A large steel or aluminum square, useful for laying out stair systems or cutting wide boards, or for checking 90-degree angles.

Furring strips: Strips of wood (or sometimes metal) attached to a basement wall or other surface to make it even, or to form an insulatable air space, or to act as a nailable base for drywall.

Fuse box: The central box that distributes electrical power throughout the house by means of fusible circuits. A fuse box should be upgraded to a breaker box, which uses circuit breakers in place of old-fashioned replaceable fuses.

Gate valve/main water shutoff: The single valve, usually at the point of the main water pipe entry into the house, that shuts off all water flowing into the plumbing supply system.

Ground-fault circuit interrupter (GFCI): A special circuit breaker or electrical socket that interrupts power almost instantly when it detects an undesirable ground such as a human body. A GFCI is useful for preventing electrocution, and is therefore required by most codes for outdoor, basement, bathroom or other applications where electricity is juxtaposed with possible water or moisture.

Hammer, drywall: A special-purpose hammer designed for installing drywall, with a slightly tilted, mushroom-shaped head and convex poll that makes a pronounced dimple in the facing of drywall.

Hammer, finish: A light (12- or 16-ounce) hammer with a smooth poll, used for trimwork.

Hammer, framing: A long-handled 20- to 32-ounce hammer for nailing framing members, usually with a checkered poll to avoid ricochets.

Hanger bars: Fixed or adjustable metal frames designed to fit between adjacent joists in order to support a junction box and light fixture.

Header: A framing member or beam placed perpendicular to joists, studs or rafters.

Joint tape: Can be paper tape or mesh tape, both used to close and join drywall joints.

Joists: The thick parallel framing members that form the floor of the first floor and ceiling of the basement.

Keyhole saw: A specialty saw with a pointy blade, once used to make keyholes, presumably, but now useful for cutting circles or rectangles, as for electrical receptacles in drywall.

Lintel: The horizontal member over a door or window, supporting the weight above it. A lintel is a header, although not all headers are lintels.

Live weight: The weight of permanent, stationary construction, human beings and furniture.

Mil: A unit of measurement, usually thickness, equal to one-thousandth of an inch.

Mudsill: Treated (rotproofed) framing members that make direct contact with concrete slabs or foundations.

Muntins: Vertical and horizontal sashbars separating the panes of a window. Also the vertical member between two panels on panelwork.

Nail set: A small punchlike tool, used in conjunction with a finish hammer, for the purpose of setting nail heads below the surface of the material being attached.

Neutral axis: The center of a framing member such as a joist, where the forces of compression are equalized. This is the correct place to drill a hole for pipes or wires.

Oakum: Hemp fiber used for caulking the joints of cast-iron soil pipe.

Panel box/breaker: See FUSE BOX.

Parging (masonry): A thin coat of masonry to smooth off concrete or block walls.

Plates: A horizontal structural member placed at the top and bottom of a wall or partition, perpendicular to other members such as the studs.

Plumb: Perpendicular to the horizon and parallel to

a line drawn through the center of the earth; straight up and down.

Plumb bob: A tool used to determine plumb by means of a string on which a pointed weight is suspended.

Rafter: One of a series of structural roof members designed to carry the weight of the roof and slanted to shed rain and snow.

Rafter square: See FRAMING SQUARE.

Reamer and bender: Specialty tools for removing burrs from and bending metal conduit during the installation of electrical wiring.

Receptacle: Also known as an electrical outlet, this device receives the two- or three-prong plugs of appliances and electrical motors. Rating is stamped on the back. Usually "hot," with current flowing to them and available for use. Installed in the finish wiring phase of a job, after rough wiring.

Reveal: The slight setback, usually ³⁄₁₆ inch, of certain finish members (such as casing) from the corner of a jamb all around its circumference. Reveals create an artistic effect, a small "shadow" that hides imperfections. Also, the gap between a door and the adjacent jamb.

Rigid copper tubing: The best-quality supply tubing for plumbing, usually in diameters of ⅜ inch to 1 inch and most commonly ½ inch. Available in various thicknesses: Type K (thick), L (medium) and M (thin). Type L is usual for residential purposes.

Rise/run: Rise is the vertical distance through which anything rises, such as a set of stairs or a roof. Run is the horizontal distance that anything runs. Rise "over" run equals the degree of incline. *Unit rise* and *unit run*, as opposed to *total* rise and run, are the individual units of rise or run that occur on a stair carriage—the distance that each step covers vertically and horizontally.

Rough opening: An unfinished opening in a wall, usually for doors and windows. The jambs go inside this "R.O.," as it is abbreviated.

Screw jacks: Construction-rated jacks operating on a screw principle, used to raise elements of a house. They're sometimes built into permanent lally columns, which are placed under bearing beams to level them out.

Sleepers: Wooden members, ranging from timbers to mere strips, placed on a slab or sometimes embedded in it, to support a finish floor.

Soffit: The underside of the elements of a building, such as the lowered part of a kitchen ceiling to which cabinets are attached, or the closed-off area under rafter tails, or any area of dropped ceiling in a basement.

Spackle: A type of water-based hard putty, used for filling cracks and holes in masonry or drywall.

Stock: Raw lumber available from a supplier, such as "2-by" stock—2x2s, 2x4s, 2x6s, 2x8s, etc.

Striker plate: The metal plate provided in a lockset that goes over the mortised hole in the jamb, into which the latch bolt slides.

Thinset: Special mortar used to adhere tiles to surfaces such as plywood. So named to distinguish it from the thick base of regular mortar that was once the standard means of setting tiles. Originally a trade name.

Thin-walled conduit: EMT (Electric Metallic Tubing) that protects house wiring in areas where it is surface-mounted. Wires are pulled through it and connected. Some local electrical codes require that even wires *inside* the walls be protected by conduit.

Toenailing: Setting a nail at an angle to attach two pieces of butt-jointed lumber, as opposed to end-nailing. Useful for attaching studs to the tops and bottoms of pre-installed plate stock.

Trimmer: The stud that goes directly under the ends of lintels over doors and windows, nailed to the king stud (the stud that is nailed to the ends of headers). Supports the weight of the header, as well as the weight of the floor above.

TSP (trisodium phosphate): A powder that is mixed with water to form an effective cleaning solution and grease solvent. Wear rubber gloves when using TSP, as it is caustic to exposed skin.

Wane: The defective area of a board that is missing material at one of the edges, usually a result of bark and the rounded surface of the tree being left intact during the milling of the lumber.

Wet wall: The wall with 2x6 or 2x8 studs that contains the plumbing for a sink, shower or tub. The extra width of material used in such a wall allows room for 4-inch pipe.

INDEX